Best Climbs
Grand Teton National Park

Mark Newcomb on the *Lower*
Exum Ridge **(III 5.7), Grand Teton.**

PHOTO GREG VON DOERSTEN

Best Climbs
Grand Teton
National Park

RICHARD ROSSITER

FALCONGUIDES

GUILFORD, CONNECTICUT
HELENA, MONTANA

AN IMPRINT OF GLOBE PEQUOT PRESS

To buy books in quantity for corporate use
or incentives, call **(800) 962-0973**
or e-mail **premiums@GlobePequot.com**.

FALCONGUIDES®

FalconGuides is an imprint of Globe Pequot Press.

Falcon, FalconGuides, and Outfit Your Mind are registered trademarks of Morris Book Publishing, LLC.

All interior photos by Richard Rossiter unless otherwise noted

Maps © Morris Book Publishing, LLC
Topos by Richard Rossiter and Sue Murray © Morris Book Publishing, LLC

Project editor: David Legere
Text design: Sheryl P. Kober
Layout: Sue Murray

Library of Congress Cataloging-in-Publication data is on file.

ISBN 978-0-7627-7338-1

Printed in China
10 9 8 7 6 5 4 3 2 1

WARNING

Climbing is a sport where you may be seriously injured or die. Read this before you use this book.

This guidebook is a compilation of unverified information gathered from many different climbers. The author cannot ensure the accuracy of any of the information in this book, including the topos and route descriptions, the difficulty ratings, and the protection ratings. These may be incorrect or misleading, as ratings of climbing difficulty and danger are always subjective and depend on the physical characteristics (for example, height), experience, technical ability, confidence, and physical fitness of the climber who supplied the rating. Additionally, climbers who achieve first ascents sometimes underrate the difficulty or danger of the climbing route. Therefore, be warned that you must exercise your own judgment on where a climbing route goes, its difficulty, and your ability to safely protect yourself from the risks of rock climbing. Examples of some of these risks are: falling due to technical difficulty or due to natural hazards such as holds breaking, falling rock, climbing equipment dropped by other climbers, hazards of weather and lightning, your own equipment failure, and failure or absence of fixed protection.

You should not depend on any information gleaned from this book for your personal safety; your safety depends on your own good judgment, based on experience and a realistic assessment of your climbing ability. If you have any doubt as to your ability to safely climb a route described in this book, do not attempt it.

The following are some ways to make your use of this book safer:

1. Consultation: You should consult with other climbers about the difficulty and danger of a particular climb prior to attempting it. Most local climbers are glad to give advice on routes in their area; we suggest that you contact locals to confirm ratings and safety of particular routes and to obtain first-hand information about a route chosen from this book.

2. Instruction: Most climbing areas have local climbing instructors and guides available. We recommend that you engage an instructor or guide to learn safety techniques and to become familiar with the routes and hazards of the areas described in this book. Even after you are proficient in climbing safely, occasional use of a guide is a safe way to raise your climbing standard and learn advanced techniques.

3. Fixed Protection: Some of the routes in this book may use bolts and pitons that are permanently placed in the rock. Because of variances in the manner of place-ment, weathering, metal fatigue, the quality of the metal used, and many other fac-tors, these fixed protection pieces should always be considered suspect and should always be backed up by equipment that you place yourself. Never depend on a single piece of fixed protection for your safety, because you never can tell whether it will hold weight. In some cases, fixed protection may have been removed or is now miss-ing. However, climbers should not always add new pieces of protection unless exist-ing protection is faulty. Existing protection can be tested by an experienced climber and its strength determined. Climbers are strongly encouraged not to add bolts and drilled pitons to a route. They need to climb the route in the style of the first ascent party (or better) or choose a route within their ability—a route to which they do not have to add additional fixed anchors.

Be aware of the following specific potential hazards that could arise in using this book:

1. Incorrect Descriptions of Routes: If you climb a route and you have a doubt as to where it goes, you should not continue unless you are sure that you can go that way safely. Route descriptions and topos in this book could be inaccurate or misleading.

2. Incorrect Difficulty Rating: A route might be more difficult than the rating indi-cates. Do not be lulled into a false sense of security by the difficulty rating.

3. Incorrect Protection Rating: If you climb a route and you are unable to arrange adequate protection from the risk of falling through the use of fixed pitons or bolts and by placing your own protection devices, do not assume that there is adequate protection available higher just because the route protection rating indicates the route does not have an X or an R rating. Every route is potentially an X (a fall may be deadly), due to the inherent hazards of climbing—including, for example, failure or absence of fixed protection, your own equipment's failure, or improper use of climb-ing equipment.

There are no warranties, whether expressed or implied, that this guidebook is accurate or that the information contained in it is reliable. There are no warranties of fitness for a particular purpose or that this guide is merchantable. Your use of this book indicates your assumption of the risk that it may contain errors and is an acknowledgment of your own sole responsibility for your climbing safety.

Contents

Grand Teton National Park

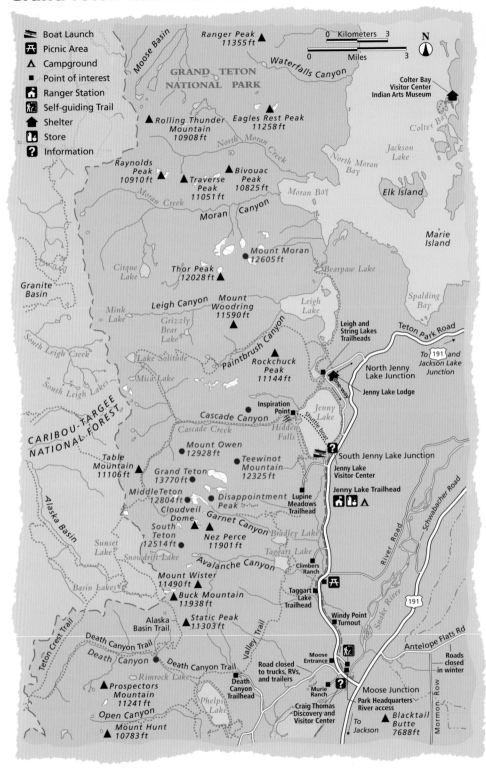

Boat Launch
Picnic Area
Campground
Point of interest
Ranger Station
Self-guiding Trail
Shelter
Store
Information

Kilometers
Miles

N

GRAND TETON NATIONAL PARK

Ranger Peak
11355ft

Moose Basin

Waterfalls Canyon

Colter Bay
Visitor Center
Indian Arts Museum

Rolling Thunder
Mountain
10908ft

Eagles Rest Peak
11258ft

North Moran Creek

Colter Bay

Jackson Lake

Raynolds Peak
10910ft

Traverse Peak
11051ft

Bivouac Peak
10825ft

North Moran Bay

Moran Bay

Elk Island

Moran Creek

Moran Canyon

Mount Moran
12605ft

Bearpaw Lake

Marie Island

Cirque Lake

Thor Peak
12028ft

Granite Basin

Leigh Canyon

Mount Woodring
11590ft

Leigh Lake

Spalding Bay

Mink Lake

Grizzly Bear Lake

Paintbrush Canyon

Rockchuck Peak
11144ft

Leigh and String Lakes Trailheads

Teton Park Road

South Leigh Creek

Lake Solitude

Mica Lake

South Leigh Lakes

To 191 and Jackson Lake Junction

North Jenny Lake Junction

One Way

Jenny Lake Lodge

CARIBOU-TARGEE NATIONAL FOREST

Cascade Canyon

Inspiration Point

Cascade Creek

Jenny Lake

Hidden Falls

Shuttle boat

Mount Owen
12928ft

Teewinot Mountain
12325ft

South Jenny Lake Junction

Table Mountain
11106ft

Grand Teton
13770ft

Jenny Lake Visitor Center

Middle Teton
12804ft

Disappointment Peak

Lupine Meadows Trailhead

Jenny Lake Trailhead

Alaska Basin

Cloudveil Dome

Garnet Canyon

Bradley Lake

River Road

Schwabacher Road

South Teton
12514ft

Nez Perce
11901ft

Sunset Lake

Snowdrift Lake

Avalanche Canyon

Taggart Lake

Basin Lakes

Mount Wister
11490ft

Climbers Ranch

Buck Mountain
11938ft

Taggart Lake Trailhead

191

Teton Crest Trail

Alaska Basin Trail

Static Peak
11303ft

Windy Point Turnout

Snake River

Antelope Flats Rd

Death Canyon Trail

Valley Trail

Death Canyon Trail

Moose Entrance

Roads closed in winter

Death Canyon

Rimrock Lake

Death Canyon Trailhead

Road closed to trucks, RVs, and trailers

Murie Ranch

Moose Junction

Mormon Row

Prospectors Mountain
11241ft

Open Canyon

Phelps Lake

Craig Thomas Discovery and Visitor Center

Park Headquarters
River access

To Jackson

Blacktail Butte
7688ft

Mount Hunt
10783ft

Acknowledgments

The information in this book is derived from my personal experience in the Tetons (1975 to present) and from the knowledge and experience of friends and associates. For providing route descriptions, first ascent data, photographs, and general expertise, I would like to thank Gene Ellis, Paul Gagner, Tim Hogan, Ted Kerasote, George Meyers, George Montopoli, and Jack Tackle. The Teton ranger staff including Jim Springer, Susan Harrington, Mark Magnuson, and Chris Harder were very helpful as were Micheal Keating and Rex Hong of Teton Mountaineering. Also thanks to Janet Lynch, executive director of the Grand Teton Association, for helping track down updated information, and to Jackson photographer Greg Von Doersten (www.gregvondoersten.com), whose climbing images light up these pages.

Climbers on the *East Ridge* route (II 5.6), Mount Owen.
PHOTO GREG VON DOERSTEN

Introduction

The Teton Range is distinguished by the unusual characteristic that, from the east, it rises very abruptly, without the typical intermediary of foothills. The lower slopes of the range, cloaked in trees and jewel-like lakes, simply fall away beneath several thousand feet of sheer rock, glaciers, and hanging snowfields that stand in stark contrast to the sage-dotted plain of Jackson Hole. The highest peak in the range, the Grand Teton, towers 7,000 feet above the floor of a valley that was once the haunt of Indians and mountain men. Most of the summits are fairly narrow with all the highest peaks lined up along the western margin of the flat valley. The ultimate effect is that of a great, impregnable wall like the Ered Nimrais in J. R. R. Tolkien's famous trilogy, *Lord of the Rings*. There are other dramatic mountain ranges in this part of the world, such as the Picket Range in the North Cascades or the Ritter Range in the Sierras, though none has the topographical isolation, vertical relief, and easy access of the Tetons.

Climbing in the Tetons offers a wide range of compelling options in an incomparable alpine setting. Routes vary from enjoyable alpine scrambles such as the *East Face* of Teewinot to high-angle rock masterpieces like the *South Buttress Right* on Mount Moran. There are the great alpine classics such as the *Black Ice Couloir* on the Grand Teton and sweeping snow climbs like the *Glacier Route* on the Middle Teton. Winter ascents in the Tetons are not uncommon, when even the easiest routes become challenging and one can expect deep snow, high winds, and extreme cold. The *Owen-Spalding* route on the Grand Teton is often climbed during winter. Several waterfalls form up, such as *Prospector Falls* and *Rimrock Falls* in Death Canyon, and provide excellent steep ice climbs.

Teton rock is generally quite solid and for the most part has good cracks. Contrary to popular notion, the peaks do not consist entirely of granite. Precambrian gneiss and schist form the core of the range with only the highest peaks from Buck Mountain to Leigh Canyon having a preponderance of granite. Even within the granite there are large, angular masses of the more ancient gneiss. Thus, on a single climb you will encounter more than one type of rock. A labyrinth of granite and pegmatite dikes runs throughout the range with massive, vertical dikes of black diabase distinguishing several of the main peaks. Teton rock provides excellent climbing with abundant holds and reasonable protection. Fixed pins and the occasional bolt are found where transient protection cannot be placed.

Equipment

Appropriate climbing hardware can vary drastically from one route to another, and for any route, what a climber chooses to bring is clearly a matter of taste and style. With this in mind, it is almost ridiculous to make suggestions. But for whatever assistance it may provide, the following gear likely would prove useful on most Teton climbs:

- RPs #2, #3, #4, and #5
- Wired stoppers up to 1 inch
- 3 or 4 TCUs
- Set of Aliens
- Various camming devices up to 3 inches
- 6 to 8 quickdraws
- 5 or 6 runners long enough to wear over the shoulder
- 7 or 8 unoccupied carabiners (typically with the runners)

Snow and ice climbs such as the *Black Ice Couloir* require crampons, ice axe(s), snow pickets, ice screws and, in some cases, a Thread as well as some part of the rock climbing gear listed above. Specific equipment suggestions are given with route descriptions.

Ratings

Climbs are rated using the Yosemite Decimal System (YDS); the topos use a slightly streamlined version, such that the Class 5 designation is assumed and the ratings 5.0 through 5.14 are written as .0 through .14 without the 5 prefix. The Welzenbach system (Germany, 1920s) is applied in part: Class 2 through Class 4 have been retained and appear on the topos as CL2, CL3 and CL4. It is worth recalling that the Yosemite Decimal System is based on the old Welzenbach grades where Class 5 refers to all climbing of sufficient difficulty to require belays and placed protection. Aid climbing or "direct aid" difficulty is written as A1 through A5 (Class 6 in the old Welzenbach grades). The difficulty of alpine snow and ice climbing is represented as AI1 through AI5. Water ice (frozen waterfalls) climbing is represented as WI1 through WI5. The Roman numerals I through VI for overall difficulty (grade) also are employed in the usual manner. No symbols are used to designate the relative safety of a climb.

At best, any rating represents a consensus of opinion from some of the climbers who have completed a route; it is still opinion and nothing more. People have debated the difficulty of climbs since the sport began and will no doubt continue to do so. Please remember that this book is only a guide to the routes; in the end it is your skill and good judgment that will keep you safe and successful on the rocks.

Doug Coombs soloing the last pitch of the *Black Ice Couloir* (IV 5.7, AI3+), Grand Teton.
PHOTO GREG VON DOERSTEN

Steel food storage box at the Meadows, Garnet Canyon.

FOOD STORAGE ONLY
SHARE BOX WITH OTHERS
LEAVE NO TRASH
CLOSE AND LATCH AFTER USE

Environmental Considerations

The magnificent landscape and fragile ecosystem of the Tetons is a precious heritage that deserves our deepest respect, appreciation, and best efforts toward preservation. Unlike parks in a more urban setting where disposable diapers, used food containers, and wadded Kleenex lurk behind every bush, the Tetons are refreshingly pristine. Off-trail foot traffic poses the greatest environmental impact related to the sport of climbing. There is the occasional food wrapper or bit of tape, but it is the long-term wear and tear of feet, especially those clad in mountain boots, that leave a lasting scar on the mountains.

To preserve the natural beauty and ecological integrity of our climbing environment, a few suggestions are offered. Deposit solid human waste at least 200 feet from water, camps, and approach paths. Do not hide it under a rock (the usual trick). Below tree line, waste can be buried with the aid of a plastic garden spade (useful and lightweight). Dig a "cat hole" 12 inches deep and cover it completely. Carry used toilet paper out in a plastic bag. Do not leave man-made material lying about. Even cigarette filters are remarkably durable. Here is the best policy: If you pack it in, pack it out.

Take care to preserve trees and other plants on approaches and climbs. Use trails and footpaths where they have been developed. Be a conscientious climber and remove obstructions, stack loose rocks along trailsides, and pick up the occasional bit of trash. While hiking across tundra, follow established paths or step on rocks to avoid crushing fragile plant life.

Fires are allowed only at campsites with fire grates. It is best, however, to use portable camp stoves for all cooking. Do not feed or interfere with birds and other animals. Bears are natural scavengers; they will tear into and eat anything that smells remotely like food.

Bear-proof food canisters are required for all overnight camping below 10,000 feet, and are provided by the park. Your best bet is to not camp below tree line at all. There is a very real risk of finding your tent and everything in it destroyed by bears when you return from your climb. This can happen even with food stored in a canister, or with no food at all. Steel boxes for food storage have been installed by the National Park Service at a few important campsites such as the Platforms, the Meadows, and Petzoldt Caves in Garnet Canyon.

Check with the National Park Service for other suggestions and regulations. Go to www.tetonclimbing.blogspot.com to learn more.

Weather and Snow Conditions

Climbing in the Tetons is done primarily from late June through September, when you can expect comfortable to hot daytime temperatures, sunny mornings, and afternoon thundershowers. Nearly every peak climb will require an ice axe and mountain boots for some part of the approach, climb, or descent

Climbing the *Owen-Spalding* route on the Grand Teton in winter.

until August. The weather is usually hot during the day, and many climbs can be done without encountering snow from late July through August, though afternoon thunderstorms are standard fare and it can still snow and be very cold. Temperatures cool a bit in September, but fair weather is likely and the climbs are still dry. The first serious snow may arrive in October, though good climbing can still be had, especially on south-facing features. It gets very cold in November and winter ice climbs begin to form up. Many peaks including the Grand Teton are climbed during the winter; climbers must anticipate arctic conditions, weeklong snowstorms, high winds, bitter cold, verglas, spindrift, and considerable adversity in accomplishing even the simplest things (such as zipping your jacket or eating). Winter climbing in the Tetons is extremely demanding and truly the province of expert mountaineers. Spring is avalanche time in the Tetons.

Log onto www.tetonclimbing.blogspot.com for current conditions and a wealth of important information during any season. This website is sponsored by Grand Teton National Park (GTNP) and the Jenny Lake Climbing Rangers. Call (307) 739-3343, 8 a.m. to 5 p.m. during the summer. Also visit www.grand.teton .national-park.com/hike.htm.

Visitor Facilities and Services

There is a campground and visitor center at Colter Bay, though climbers will be primarily interested in the visitor center at Moose and the rustic ranger station at Jenny Lake. The rangers who work at this location are experienced Teton climbers and have a wealth of practical information for the asking. Maps are available at Colter Bay, Moose and the Jenny Lake Visitor Center (you need a map).

Nearly all climbing activity begins and ends at the Jenny Lake Ranger Station (during the summer), not only for its strategic proximity to the main peaks, but also because a backcountry permit is required for overnight outings and you can speak with a climbing ranger in person. Registration for day climbs is voluntary. All overnight camping below 10,000 feet requires the use of bear-proof food canisters and a backcountry permit. GTNP has an expert mountain rescue team and will conduct rescues if needed.

The most strategic campground for climbers is at Jenny Lake (see also Gros Ventre and Signal Mountain Campgrounds). There are many other facilities inside the park. The town of Jackson offers good restaurants, laundromats, outdoor shops such as Teton Mountaineering, and way too much to list here. Stop at the Jackson Chamber of Commerce for a map of town and a list of services. The best source for climbing information is the Jenny Lake Ranger Station (307-739-3343).

The Climber's Ranch, operated by the American Alpine Club, is located 4 miles north of Moose on the west side of Teton Park Road. The ranch offers overnight accommodations and showers at very reasonable rates. Bring your own sleeping bag, towels, and cook gear. The ranch is open from June 11 to September 11. Mail, call, or e-mail Grand Teton Climbers' Ranch, P.O. Box 57, Moose WY 83012; (307) 733-7271 (June 1 to September 30 only); www.friendsofgtcr.net.

Getting to the Tetons

US 191 is the main road going north through the town of Jackson, Wyoming. To reach Moose and Jenny Lake from US 191, turn west at Moose Junction onto Teton Park Road. The first turn on the right leads to Dornan's, which features a climbing shop, mountain bike rental, grocery store, canoe rental, liquor store, bar/lounge, gas station, and other conveniences. Continue west on Teton Park Road. Find the Craig Thomas Discovery and Visitor Center on the left and the post office on the right. Pass through an entrance station; a daily fee or annual pass is required to enter GTNP. Pick up a park map and a copy of the *Grand Teton Guide* (a park tabloid with much useful information).

Follow the road as it bends around to head north, and after 7 super-scenic miles, turn left at South Jenny Lake Junction. Another quarter mile or so leads to the Jenny Lake Visitor Center, Ranger Station, shuttle boat dock, Jenny Lake Campground, trailhead for the Jenny Lake Trail and the Valley Trail, and Jenny Lake. Printable maps can be downloaded at www.nps.gov/grte/planyourvisit/ hike.htm.

Using This Guide

This book is intended for the experienced climber; it is not a manual of instruction, but a guide to the routes. It assumes that the reader is already proficient in the placement of climbing hardware, the use of a rope, and has climbed before in the mountains. Whereas this book contains much useful information, it cannot take the place of skill and good judgment. Take care in planning an ascent. Be sure to have proper gear and clothing. Allow adequate time to complete the route; an unplanned night on the peaks can have serious consequences. Teton weather can deteriorate rapidly, and warm, sunny weather in the morning can turn into a violent storm by early afternoon (a common pattern). Rockfall can occur on any route at any time. Regardless of your level of experience, if the situation in which you find yourself does not look good, consider retreat. You can always return another day.

Two climbing schools are authorized by GTNP and are available for those who seek the instruction or service of a guide. These can be found at www .tetonclimbing.blogspot.com.

Topo Legend

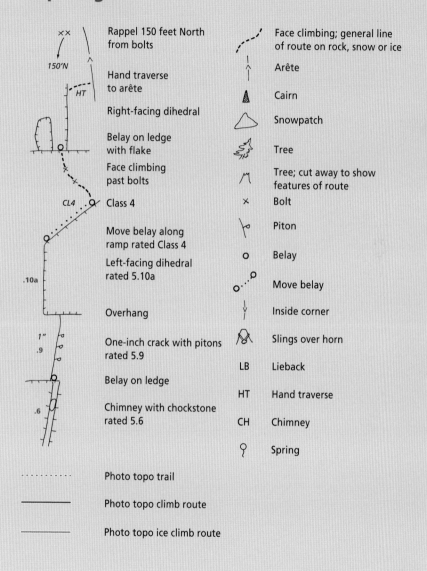

Rappel 150 feet North from bolts

Hand traverse to arête

Right-facing dihedral

Belay on ledge with flake

Face climbing past bolts

Class 4

Move belay along ramp rated Class 4

Left-facing dihedral rated 5.10a

Overhang

One-inch crack with pitons rated 5.9

Belay on ledge

Chimney with chockstone rated 5.6

Face climbing; general line of route on rock, snow or ice

Arête

Cairn

Snowpatch

Tree

Tree; cut away to show features of route

Bolt

Piton

Belay

Move belay

Inside corner

Slings over horn

LB   Lieback

HT   Hand traverse

CH   Chimney

Spring

Photo topo trail

Photo topo climb route

Photo topo ice climb route

**Jeff Splittgerber on the second pitch
of *Prospector Falls,* winter 1976.**

1.

Death Canyon

Death Canyon is the third major drainage north from the southern margin of Grand Teton National Park. This deep, glacier-carved valley is a popular approach to the Teton Crest Trail and presents some of the best crag climbing in the range. The main attraction during summer is Cathedral Rock, the 1,000-foot southwest buttress of Point 10,552 (Albright Peak). The canyon provides a fine ski tour and several excellent ice climbs during winter.

Getting there: To reach Death Canyon from Moose Junction, drive 3 miles south on Moose-Wilson Road. Turn right at a signed junction and drive about 0.7 mile to where a right branch goes to White Grass Ranch (now closed). Bear left and continue for about a mile to a parking area at White Grass Ranger Station and the end of the road. The first mile of Death Canyon Road is paved, but the second mile becomes quite rough, and a high-clearance vehicle is recommended to reach the trailhead. This road is not plowed during winter.

Aerial view of Death Canyon from the West

Approach Routes Viewed from the Southeast

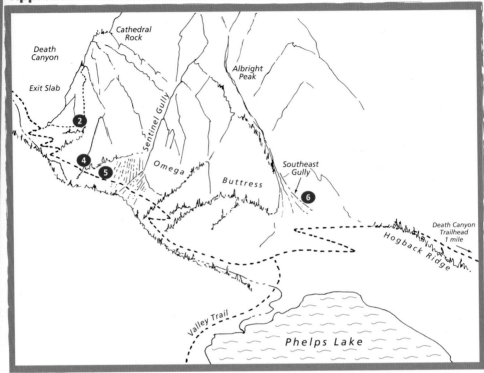

TRAILS

Valley Trail

This important trail runs on a north-south axis all the way from Teton Village to Trapper Lake. Some length of the Valley Trail must be hiked to reach most of the trails and destinations described in this guidebook. Granite Canyon Trailhead is the access point farthest south within Grand Teton National Park. The Valley Trail may also be accessed from the Taggart Lake, Death Canyon, Lupine Meadows,

Jenny Lake, String Lake, and Leigh Lake Trailheads.

Death Canyon Trail

This trail begins at the end of the road and soon joins the Valley Trail (go left). It climbs gently for about 1.4 miles to a scenic shoulder above Phelps Lake, then descends across a talus slope into the narrows of Death Canyon where the Valley Trail goes left (stay right). Sentinel Turret appears up the canyon as the steep tower on the north side. A level stretch in the forested valley

Descent Routes Viewed from the West

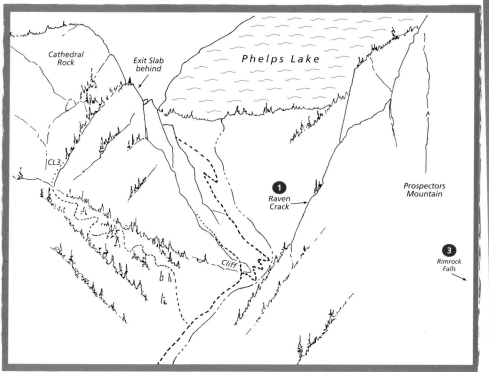

leads to two switchbacks that place the trail higher on the north slope. A long, gentle stretch passes beneath Omega Buttress, Sentinel Gully, and Sentinel Turret, beyond which the trail climbs more steeply via eight switchbacks directly beneath Cathedral Rock. A footpath climbs back to the northeast from the last switchback and leads to the beginning of the routes on Cathedral Rock. The main trail levels off a short way beyond this point and 3.9 miles from the trailhead reaches a patrol cabin and a junction with the Alaska Basin Trail. The canyon opens up and the trail climbs gently for a couple of miles beneath the north and west sides of Prospectors Mountain. A final series of switchbacks leads to Fox Creek Pass and a junction with the Teton Crest Trail.

PROSPECTORS MOUNTAIN

Winter Ice Climbs
Prospectors Mountain (11,241 feet) rises to the west of Phelps Lake and forms the south side of Death Canyon.

Death Canyon from the East in Winter

It holds several alpine tarns and has a very rugged northeast face across Death Canyon from Cathedral Rock.

1. Prospector Falls (IV WI4) This is the large and obvious frozen waterfall on the northeast face of Prospectors Mountain across Death Canyon from the Sentinel Turret. It is also known as Raven Falls or Raven Crack Falls for its proximity to a rock climb of the same name. The climb consists of four pitches of ice with the second and fourth pitches being the most diffi-cult. Some parties complete only the first two pitches. Skis or snowshoes are needed for the approach by the time the ice is well formed, usually by December. The route was first climbed by Dave and Peter Carmen during the early 1970s.

Approach: Follow the Death Canyon Trail until it nears the stream below Cathedral Rock (about 2 miles), then cross the drainage and head south to the bottom of the falls (all very obvious once you're there).

The Route
Pitch 1: Climb a 50-foot bulge and belay on an ice ledge. **Pitch 2:** Tackle the 150-foot vertical section and belay where the angle eases. **Pitch 3:** Do an easy pitch up to the left, then curve back right and belay at the base of the final steep section. **Pitch 4:**

Climb 100 feet of steep ice to a large bench.

Rack: Ice screws and ice tools. Thread not required.

Descent: Make several long rappels from trees to the west of the falls.

2. The Nugget (WI4+) This is a steep smear immediately west of Prospector Falls on the south side of the big gully. It is visible from the approach. Beware of avalanches.

3. Rimrock Falls (III WI4) Rimrock Lake is a secluded tarn high on the north face of Prospectors Mountain about 2,000 feet above the Death Canyon Trail. The cascade that descends northward from the lake provides about 900 feet of ice climbing in three sections of ascending difficulty. The first ascent was made by Jeff Splittgerber and Richard Rossiter on February 20, 1977. The ice is best during mid to late winter. Skis or snowshoes are needed for the approach.

Approach: Hike (ski) the Death Canyon Trail about 2 miles beyond Cathedral Rock to where the trail crosses to the left side of the main stream. *Rimrock Falls* will be seen

Prospector Falls Ice Climb

directly to the south. The first section of ice is about 300 yards south of the trail.

The Route
Section 1: Climb about 175 feet of variable ice up to 55 degrees, then slog 300 feet of snow and/or slabby ice. **Section 2:** Do three long leads over ice slabs and bulges up to 60 degrees. Climb about 500 feet of snow with some ice bulges and belay

at the base of the final steep section. **Section 3:** Climb two magnificent pitches of blue-green ice from 70 to 90 degrees and arrive in the hanging cirque of Rimrock Lake.

Descent: Slog down the broad gully to the west of the upper formation, then follow the main couloir until it steepens. Traverse northeast and rappel from trees to easy terrain.

ALBRIGHT PEAK (POINT 10,552)

Albright Peak is a modest summit along the south ridge of Static Peak, named Point 10,552 on the USGS Grand Teton Quadrangle (1968). It would go mostly unnoticed except that its south face forms the very spectacular north wall at the entrance to Death Canyon. Its prominent features include (from west to east) Cathedral Rock, Sentinel Turret, Sentinel Gully, and Omega Buttress.

Winter Ice Climbs

There are several ice climbs along the north side of Death Canyon that face south into the winter sun and as a consequence are somewhat transitory. The following two climbs are pretty good when the ice is in, but even then they are only "Temporary Like Achilles."

4. Sentinel Ice Couloir (III WI4) This is not to be confused with the large drainage between Sentinel Turret and Omega Buttress that is called Sentinel Gully. The ice climb ascends the steep couloir on the west side of Sentinel Turret and consists of three or four pitches of ice. Wallow up snow for about 300 feet to reach the ice. A 40-foot pillar on the third pitch is the crux; this can be passed more easily to the left.

Descent: Rappel from fixed anchors.

5. Dread Fall (III 5.10a WI5) This transient formation is probably the most difficult ice climb in Death Canyon. It begins directly above the trail about 100 yards west from Sentinel Gully.

The Route

Pitch 1: Mixed climbing leads up and left through the initial cliff. **Pitch 2:** Climb up and right over thin, low-angle ice (WI3). **Pitch 3:** Climb an ice pillar on the left or a difficult mixed chimney on the right. **Pitch 4:** A final short pitch leads to a ledge (WI3).

Rack: Bring a selection of ice screws, several LAs and small angles, and #1 to #3 Friends.

Descent: Walk west on a ledge and rappel 150 feet from fixed pins and slings wrapped around a block to a snow bench. Walk west about 50 yards, then angle down to the trail.

6. Southeast Gully Routes (I WI2–3) Four or five short ice climbs form above the Death Canyon Trail to the northwest of Phelps Lake (above the Valley Trail junction). The longest of these, the *Battle of the Buldge* (WI3), is about 150 feet high. These are not Teton classics by any stretch of the imagination, but are good warm-ups for their big brothers up the canyon.

CATHEDRAL ROCK

Cathedral Rock is the farthest west and most impressive of the major buttresses on the south side of Point 10,552. This beautiful feature, more a "wall" than a "rock," looms up dramatically on the north as you hike through the narrows of Death Canyon. There are several good routes on this very steep wall, of which *The Snaz* and *Caveat Emptor* stand out as the great classic lines.

Approach: Hike the Death Canyon Trail to the last of eight switchbacks beneath the southwest corner of Cathedral Wall. Take a steep path that cuts back to the right. Climb a short cliff (Class 4) and follow the path east to its end beneath the middle of the wall. The cliff near the beginning of this path is unpleasant to descend, especially if wet. The standard downclimb does not return to the base of the main wall, so you may want to stash extraneous gear near the end of the downclimb instead of bringing it up to the beginning of the route.

For those unfamiliar with Cathedral Rock (and those wishing to stash gear), it is a good idea to continue up

South Face of Cathedral Rock from Death Canyon Trail

Cathedral Rock—*Caveat Emptor* and *The Snaz*

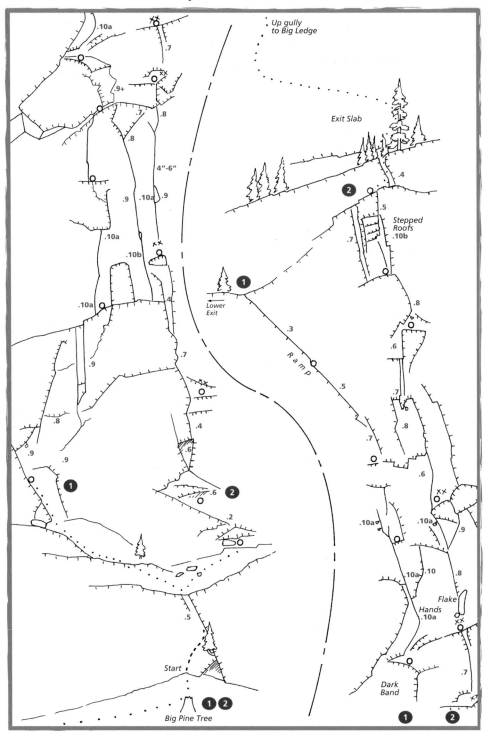

the main trail to where the southwest side of the cliff can be viewed. The downclimb follows the forested ledge that begins on the right skyline, and makes a diagonal down and left across the face to the forest/talus slope where a path leads down through trees and talus to the Death Canyon Trail, not far from the patrol cabin.

1. Caveat Emptor (III 5.10a) "Let the buyer beware," says the Latin idiom. That the climb deserves such an ominous designation is subject to question; however, those accustomed to the uncertainty of first ascents may find meaning in the name.

This great climb runs parallel on the left and near to *The Snaz,* but is harder and more sustained in difficulty. The first ascent is credited to Jim Beyer and Buck Tilley, who climbed the route as it is described here during July 1979; a number of others had climbed parts of the route previously.

Approach: Take the climber's path to a large tree beneath an immense open-book dihedral that runs up the center of the wall.

The Route
Pitch 1: Climb the initial pitch of *The Snaz* to get up onto the big, grassy ledge (5.5), then angle up and left on ramps and ledges (5.4) to the base of a left-leaning chimney (200 feet). **Pitch 2:** Start up the chimney to a fixed pin, hand traverse right (5.10a)

to a crack, and climb straight up (5.9) to a right-facing corner. Work up the corner, then angle right to belay on a ledge beside a large pillar (130 feet). **Pitch 3:** To the left of the pillar, climb a beautiful finger and hand crack up to a roof (5.10a). Turn the roof on the right (5.10a) and reach a ledge after about 30 feet (possible belay). Continue up a perfect crack (5.7) and belay on a ledge beneath a band of dark rock (165 feet overall). **Pitch 4:** Move right, make difficult moves up through a roof (5.10a), and belay across from the detached flake on the sixth pitch of *The Snaz* (90 feet). **Pitch 5:** Power up through an overhanging hand crack (5.10a), up through a left-facing corner and roof (5.10a), and belay on a ledge that is below and right of some fixed protection (150 feet). **Pitch 6:** Move up and left about 10 feet to a fixed pin, straight up past a bashie (5.10a), back right to a left-facing corner, and up to a belay ledge (90 feet). **Pitch 7:** Climb an unprotected face (5.6), then follow a left-angling ramp to a ledge (150 feet). **Pitch 8:** Work up and left along easier terrain to the base of the broad slab above *The Snaz.*

Rack: Up to 4 inches with extra pieces from 1 inch up.

Descent: Climb up and left across the slab to the big forested ledge or work straight left. See descent for *The Snaz* (below). It is possible to rappel the route from the top of pitch 6 with double 60-meter ropes. The first rappel goes down to the top of pitch 5. The next rappel requires a slight swing into *The Snaz* even with top of pitch 4. Three more long rappels lead down to the tree on the common approach pitch. A single-rope rappel takes you to the bottom of the wall.

2. The Snaz (III 5.10a) What exactly is a "snaz"? For an answer we would have to ask Yvon Chouinard, who with Mort Hempel made the first ascent on August 4, 1964. The *Stepped Roof* alternative on the last pitch was first climbed by Richard and Joyce Rossiter in August 1990. Fine steep rock, a warm southern exposure, and a relatively easy approach and descent combine to make *The Snaz* one of the most popular pure rock climbs in the Tetons. All the belays are on good ledges, and pitches 2 through 7 have fixed anchors with rappel rings. The protection is good on all pitches including variations.

   Approach: Take the climber's path to a large tree beneath an immense open-book dihedral that runs up the center of the wall. Step up to the highest ground and belay at a slab beneath a small left-facing corner with a tree.

The Route

Pitch 1: Climb up and right into the corner and work up to a broad grassy ledge (5.5). Run the rope out and belay beneath or just above a blocky overhang (5.6). **Pitch 2:** Work up a steep, not too clean, left-facing corner, then move right and up to a belay at the bottom of another left-facing dihedral (5.7). **Pitch 3:** Follow the dihedral up through a wide slot and continue up to a good stance beneath an off-width crack with a wedged block (5.7). **Pitch 4:** Jam up around the right side of the block (5.9) and continue up the long, wide crack (5.8 or 5.9) to a roof that is turned on the left (5.8). **Pitch 5:** From the stance above the roof, climb an easy crack and corner to a ledge beneath a large detached flake (5.7). **Pitch 6:** This is a great pitch. Work up past a loose block and around the left side of the flake, continue up the fist crack (5.8), then jam and stem out a magnificent overhanging crack to yet another good ledge (5.10a). It is possible (but not recommended) to avoid the overhang by working around it on the right (5.9). **Pitch 7:** Work straight up a steep dihedral (5.7) for about 60 feet, traverse left to the far side of a hanging block (5.7), then work up through the roof, up short double cracks to a ledge (5.7), and up a crack on the right to a sloping ledge in an alcove. **Pitch 8:** Make tricky moves up into a bomb-bay chimney (5.8) and follow it until it is possible to step left around an arête to a big ledge. **Pitch 9:** The traditional last pitch takes the double crack and chimney on the left to another ledge (5.7). For a more climactic, but well-protected finish, undercling and lieback out the huge, stepped roof on the right and arrive at the same belay ledge (5.10b).

Rack: Up to 4 inches with extra pieces from 1 inch up.

Descent: One must go up to go down. Scramble up the chimney above the belay (5.5) to a ledge with trees. Move right (east) to the largest tree and climb up onto a broad, smooth slab that is slippery when wet. The objective is to reach the higher, forested ledge. Climb straight up the slab to the ledge (Class 4) or, perhaps less difficult, climb up about 60 feet to a small rounded ledge and follow this west for about 300 feet (Class 3) until it is easy to gain the forested ledge. Once on the ledge, hike west about 400 feet to a three-stone cairn, then descend a gully and chimney system down across the southwest face of Cathedral Rock to the talus (Class 3). A series of crude switchbacks (please use them) lead down through the trees to open talus where a few hundred feet of boulder-hopping bring you to the level section of the trail above the eighth switchback. It may also be possible to go straight west from the last belay of *The Snaz* or *Caveat Emptor* and descend along a lower series of ledges and gullies.

Paul Gagner on Pitch 1 of Caveat Emptor.
PHOTO PAUL GAGNER COLLECTION

Central Tetons

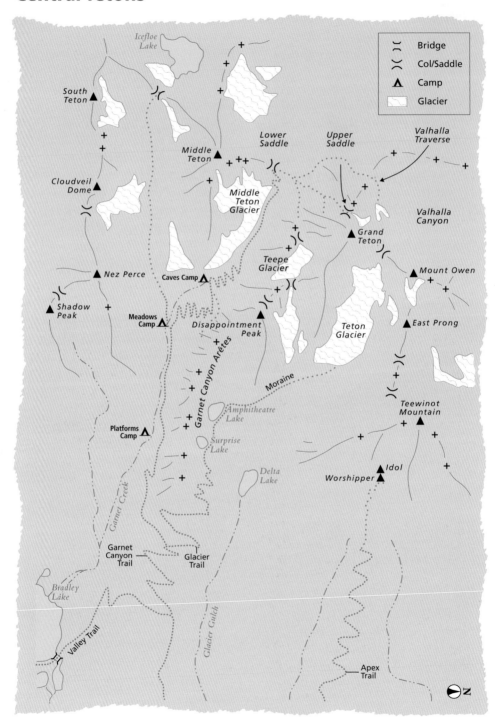

Legend:
- ‿ Bridge
- ﹀ Col/Saddle
- ▲ Camp
- Glacier

Icefloe Lake

South Teton ▲

Lower Saddle

Upper Saddle

Valhalla Traverse

Middle Teton ▲

Cloudveil Dome ▲

Middle Teton Glacier

Valhalla Canyon

Grand Teton ▲

Teepe Glacier

Nez Perce ▲

Caves Camp ▲

Mount Owen ▲

Shadow Peak ▲

Meadows Camp ▲

Disappointment Peak ▲

East Prong ▲

Teton Glacier

Garnet Canyon Arêtes

Moraine

Teewinot Mountain ▲

Amphitheatre Lake

Platforms Camp ▲

Surprise Lake

Delta Lake

Worshipper ▲   Idol ▲

Garnet Creek

Garnet Canyon Trail

Glacier Trail

Bradley Lake

Valley Trail

Glacier Gulch

Apex Trail

N

2.

Central Tetons

The great peaks of the Central Tetons are literally surrounded and isolated from the other peaks of the range by Avalanche Canyon on the south and Cascade Canyon on the north and west. These two very long canyons wrap around the Central Tetons to meet at an unnamed pass (10,560+ feet) between The Wall and the West Ridge of the South Teton. The Grand Teton dominates this island of high peaks as it dominates the entire Teton Range, and the state of Wyoming for that matter. Other peaks included in the Central Tetons are the South Teton, the Middle Teton, Mount Owen, Disappointment Peak, and Teewinot Mountain.

TRAILS AND APPROACHES

Valley Trail and
Garnet Canyon Trail

The Valley Trail begins from the Lupine Meadows Trailhead at the south end of the Lupine Meadows Parking Area (6,732 feet). It reaches a junction at 1.7 miles and goes left (south) to Bradley Lake and Taggart Lake. The Garnet Canyon Trail goes right, makes long switchbacks up the east slope of Disappointment Peak and reaches a junction with the

Amphitheater Lake Trail in another 1.3 miles. The Garnet Canyon Trail goes left at the junction, contours around into Garnet Canyon, and reaches its official end as it first draws near Garnet Creek (about 8,960 feet). This point is 1.1 miles from the previous junction and 4.1 miles from the trailhead. A good campsite called the Platforms is located on the south side of the stream.

Climbers' Trail

The more rugged Climbers' Trail begins a few yards north of Garnet Creek in some big boulders, then continues along the right side of the creek to an open area called the Meadows (campsite, about 9,250 feet). The Middle Teton rises to the west and divides the canyon into north and south forks. The Climbers' Trail takes the north fork, makes a series of short switchbacks up a steep slope, then goes west above Spalding Falls to Petzoldt Caves (campsite). More switchbacks climb to a point just below Fairshare Tower where the trail leads west along the lateral moraine of the Middle Teton Glacier to the final steep headwall below the Lower Saddle. The headwall may be ascended directly on snow in early season or via rocks to the right where a heavy rope is anchored as a handrail. From the top of the cliff, a good path climbs south and reaches the Lower Saddle (about 11,650 feet), 7 miles from the Lupine Meadows Trailhead with a total elevation gain of 4,800 feet.

Amphitheater Lake Trail (aka Glacier Trail)

This good trail begins at a signed junction 3 miles up the Garnet Canyon Trail, at the sixth (and very short) switchback on the east face of Disappointment Peak. The Glacier Trail continues straight ahead where the Garnet Canyon Trail cuts back to the left and, after nineteen switchbacks, reaches Surprise Lake at 1.6 miles and Amphitheater Lake (9,698 feet), 1.8 miles from the junction. A climber's path leads north from here to a small pass along the east ridge of Disappointment Peak. Descend 150 feet to the north, then traverse west beneath the north face of Disappointment Peak into Glacier Gulch. This traverse requires an ice axe until midsummer. A strategic campsite is found here in the moraine beneath the east ridge of the Grand Teton that provides access to the *East Ridge, North Face,* and *North Ridge* of the Grand Teton and to routes on Mount Owen and Teewinot. The Teton Glacier lies to the northwest behind its enormous terminal moraine.

Valhalla Canyon

The only other practical approach to the Grand Teton and the west side of

Mount Owen is from the north out of Cascade Canyon. This approach provides access to all routes from the *North Ridge* to the *Enclosure Ice Couloir.* Hike about 3 miles up the Cascade Canyon Trail (see the chapter on Cascade Canyon Crags) to a point just west of the drainage from Valhalla Canyon. The northwest side of the Grand Teton is visible from here. Ford Cascade Creek (a log crossing may be available a bit upstream from the confluence) and follow a rugged climber's path up the steep, forested slope, staying to the right of the stream, into Valhalla Canyon. Camp on snow or (in late season) use stone enclosures that have been built in the upper reaches of the canyon. A good platform is located just left of West Gunsight Couloir, below a small rib that descends from the west face of Mount Owen (about 11,000 feet). Water may be available in the West Gunsight Couloir.

Valhalla Traverse

A notable alternative for reaching these remote, north-facing routes is the Valhalla Traverse, the long ledge system that, without significant obstruction, traverses the entire west side of the Grand Teton and connects the Lower Saddle with upper Valhalla Canyon. Since the only reasonable descent from the summit returns to the Lower Saddle via the *Owen-Spalding* route, you may, for example, camp at the Lower Saddle, take the Valhalla Traverse, climb the *Black Ice*

Couloir or *North Ridge,* and return to camp without having to carry bivouac gear up the route.

To locate the Valhalla Traverse from the Lower Saddle, look north toward the Grand Teton and identify a cairn on a level section of the southwest ridge that is slightly higher than the Lower Saddle. This cairn marks the beginning of the scree ledge that runs across the west face of the Enclosure. Hike north from the Lower Saddle about halfway to the Black Dike, cut left on a faint path, and descend into a scree gully of reddish rock. Cross the gully, go past two small ribs, and make an ascending traverse to the level section of the southwest ridge with the cairn. A faint trail exists in this area when it is free of snow. Follow a broad ledge system across the west face of the Enclosure to the northwest ridge (good bivouac site).

Continue 100 feet around to the north side. After a short descent (about 20 feet), choose either the upper or lower version of the traverse. The upper route crosses a bowl (on snow or ice) and contours around into the *Enclosure Ice Couloir,* beyond which are two ledges: The lower ledge leads around and up into the *Black Ice Couloir.* The upper ledge leads to the north buttress of the Enclosure. The lower route descends across the bottom of the bowl and follows a snow- or ice-covered ramp down into the Second Icefield of the *Black Ice Couloir.* This option is used to reach the *North Ridge* or the original version of the *Black Ice Couloir* via ramps that diagonal up across the lower northwest face of the Grand Teton.

The Valhalla Traverse, discovered in 1960 by Leigh and Irene Ortenburger, is not a trivial undertaking.

Northwest side of the Grand Teton as seen from upper Valhalla Canyon after a snowstorm in early Ju

Mountain boots, ice axe, and crampons are needed for the traverse on the north side of the Enclosure—if not the whole thing.

CAMPSITES

Specific areas are sanctioned by the Park Service for camping, and occupancy is limited. The first and lowest campsite in Garnet Canyon is the Platforms (about 8,960 feet), located on the south side of Garnet Creek where the Garnet Canyon Trail first comes near the stream (4.1 miles from the Lupine Meadows Trailhead). Several good sites are found at the Meadows (about 9,250 feet), the beautiful, open area of Garnet Canyon immediately east of the Middle Teton, where the

canyon splits into north and south forks (4.7 miles from the trailhead). At about 5.5 miles, after a series of short, steep switchbacks, is the Caves or Petzoldt Caves (about 10,100 feet), which are actually dugouts under huge boulders. Beginning at about 6.2 miles is the Moraine Camp area (10,600 to 11,000 feet) where a series of stone enclosures or flattened areas have been built along the lateral moraine of the Middle Teton Glacier. The highest and perhaps most strategic campsite is the Lower Saddle (about 11,650 feet). This scenic perch provides an easier shot at the summit of the Grand Teton, but is often cold, windy and is 7 long, hard miles from the trailhead. Camping is also

Central Tetons from the Southeast

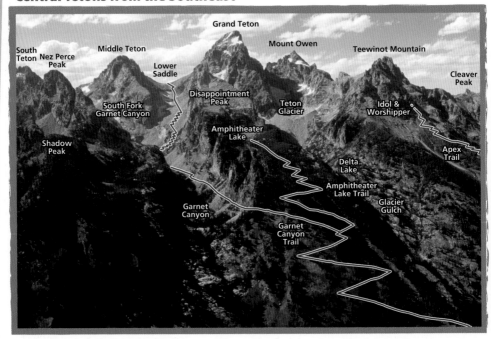

The Meadows in Garnet Canyon

allowed in the South Fork of Garnet Canyon (10,000 to 11,300 feet). Three campsites are available just north of Surprise Lake and a bivouac can be made in Glacier Gulch (10,000 feet) below the east ridge of the Grand Teton. Camps or bivouacs are also allowed in Valhalla Canyon and on the west side of the Valhalla Traverse. Check with the Jenny Lake rangers on water, snow conditions, bear issues, and availability of campsites.

South Teton

The South Teton (12,514 feet) sits at the southwest extreme of the Central Tetons, reigning above both Avalanche Canyon and Cascade Canyon. It is the southern summit of Les Trois Tetons, a historic phrase that refers to the prominence of the South Teton, Middle Teton, and Grand Teton as seen from the plains in Jackson Hole. Nez Perce, Mount Owen, and Teewinot Mountain, however, hardly go unnoticed from this perspective. The South Teton is among the easiest of the major summits in the range by either the *Northwest Couloir* or the *West Ridge* routes.

1. Northwest Couloir (I Class 4) This popular route, also known as the *Regular Route,* was first climbed by Albert Ellingwood and Eleanor Davis on August 29, 1923.

Approach: Begin from the Lupine Meadows Parking Area. Hike the Valley Trail and Garnet Canyon Trail to the Meadows, cross the stream and follow a climber's path up the South Fork of Garnet Canyon to the

South Teton from the North

saddle between the South and Middle Tetons (11,360+ feet).

The Route
Look for a vague path in the talus. Make an ascending traverse across the east slope of the ridge, then gain the ridge crest and follow it to the north face of the west ridge. Traverse left to a short couloir (snow) and climb it to the crest of the west ridge. An easy scramble leads east to the summit. It is possible in early to mid-summer to angle up and left across the north face on snow and avoid hiking all the way to the saddle.

Rack: An ice axe and mountain boots are useful even in late season.

Descent: Reverse the route.

Middle Teton

The Middle Teton (12,804) is the third-highest peak in the range and is host to a variety of excellent routes. The *Southwest Couloir* is one of the more frequented Teton scrambles, while the Middle Teton Glacier (*Glacier Route*) and the *Northwest Ice Couloir* provide sweeping ascents on classic alpine terrain. The view from the summit is simply spectacular and yields an excellent reconnaissance of the south side of the Grand Teton. The summit first was reached via the *Ellingwood Couloir* on August 29, 1923, by Albert Ellingwood, Eleanor Davis and E. W. Harnden.

Looking south from the Lower Saddle, two pinnacles can be seen low on the north ridge: Pinocchio Pinnacle is the nearer; the taller and slightly farther is Bonney's Pinnacle. Beyond these the north ridge climbs directly to the summit, passing en route a lesser protuberance called the North Peak and a notch created by an eroded diabase dike. The *Northwest Ice Couloir* climbs steeply just west of the north ridge to a notch in the west ridge near the summit. The northwest face and west ridge are seldom visited by climbers. The unnamed saddle between the Middle Teton and South Teton (11,360+ feet) lies southwest of the summit and overlooks Icefloe Lake (10,652 feet) below to the west. The *Southwest Couloir* begins from

this saddle and climbs northeast to the north summit.

The rugged south face rises above the South Fork of Garnet Canyon in a series of ridges and gullies, among which the *Ellingwood Couloir* climbs to the col above Dike Pinnacle, a minor summit on the east ridge. The east ridge begins above the Meadows in Garnet Canyon and culminates in the Dike Pinnacle (about 12,400 feet), then drops down to a col and an east-facing headwall that sweeps up to the summits. A prominent diabase dike splits the east ridge and the right side of Dike Pinnacle, then climbs to a notch in the north ridge that delineates the North Peak. The Middle Teton Glacier spans the peak from the east ridge to the north ridge and climbs in a narrow phalanx of snow and ice to the col between the Dike Pinnacle and the south summit.

Descent: The descent from the summit is the same for all routes: Scramble down the *Southwest Couloir* into the South Fork of Garnet Canyon or downclimb the *North Ridge* to the Lower Saddle.

1. Glacier Route (III 5.4, AI2+) This classic route ascends the Middle Teton Glacier to the col above the Dike Pinnacle then climbs steep snow and slabs up the east-facing headwall to the summit. In early

Middle Teton and Adjacent Peaks from the North

season this is one of the few pure glacier and snow climbs in the Tetons. One should expect some moderate rock climbing on the head-wall by mid-summer.

Rack: An ice axe, crampons and mountain boots are essential as well as a minimal rock climbing rack. Snow flukes or pickets may be useful for belays on the steeper sections. The route was first climbed on August 4, 1944 by Sterling Hendricks and Paul Bradt.

Approach: Hike the Garnet Canyon Trail and Climbers' Trail (see under Central Tetons, page 13) to about 10,800 feet where the col west of Dike

Pinnacle comes into view and it is obvious to cut south onto the broad apron of the Middle Teton Glacier.

The Route

Work up and left around the bergschrund and ascend a steep snow gully directly to the col at the west side of Dike Pinnacle. The south summit appears as a narrow tower on the left skyline. Climb steep snow and rock as necessary and gain the notch to the right of the south summit. Move right and climb moderate rock to the north summit. It is also possible to climb directly up the steep snow gully out right from the Dike Col and gain a

Middle Teton from the West

notch in the north ridge. Traverse slabs south from the notch until it is easy to climb west to the summit. Avoid any temptation to climb the south summit as there is no simple way to traverse from it to the north summit and the *Southwest Couloir* descent.

2. North Ridge (III 5.6) This route has character and takes an almost direct line from the Lower Saddle to the summit of the Middle Teton. It was first climbed by Robert Underhill and Fritiof Fryxell on July 17, 1931.

    Approach: Hike the Garnet Canyon Trail and Climbers' Trail to the Lower Saddle (see page 13).

The Route

Hike south to the base of two small rock towers: Pinocchio Pinnacle (the nearer) and Bonney's Pinnacle (the higher of the two). Pass Pinocchio on the west, climb through a notch, and pass Bonney's on the east to arrive at a deep notch formed by an eroded diabase dike. Follow a ledge around toward the left side of the ridge, then go right on another ledge to a recess in the ridge called "The Room." Climb a diagonal shelf that leads up and around the corner to the right. Continue up along the right side of the ridge, not far above the *Northwest Ice Couloir,* to the

Black Dike, and scramble to near its top. Climb over blocks to the crest (5.6) and look for a belay bolt. Easy slabs and ledges on the east side lead to the summit.

Rack: Light rock rack up to 2 inches.

3. Northwest Ice Couloir (III 5.6 AI3) The *Northwest Ice Couloir* is a first-class, if moderate, alpine climb. Peter Lev and James Greig made the first ascent on June 16, 1961. The couloir will be packed with snow in early season, but a fine ice climb is revealed after the seasonal snow has melted off. This hanging couloir lies to the right of the north ridge and finishes at a notch on the west ridge very near the north summit. The couloir is narrow at the bottom and top and reaches an angle of approximately 55 degrees.

Approach: Hike the Garnet Canyon Trail and Climbers' Trail to the Lower Saddle (see under Central Tetons, page 13).

Climbers on the *Northwest Ice Couloir* **(III 5.6 AI3), Middle Teton.**
PHOTO GREG VON DOERSTEN

The Route

Hike south to the base of two small rock towers: Pinocchio Pinnacle (the nearer) and Bonney's Pinnacle (the higher of the two). Pass Pinocchio on the west, climb through a notch, and pass Bonney's on the east to arrive at a deep notch formed by an eroded dike. Work up to the left, then back to the right and follow a ledge around into the couloir. About 700 feet of ice (or snow) lead to a notch on the west ridge from which an easy scramble leads to the north summit.

Rack: Ice tools. A few ice screws and a light rock rack are recommended.

4. Southwest Couloir (II Class 3) The *Southwest Couloir* of the Middle Teton is one of the most popular scrambles in the Teton Range. It is also the easiest way to descend from the summit. In early season the couloir yields a fine, moderate snow climb, but by August it is a long hike up talus with a bit of scrambling in the steep upper section. The route was first climbed by H. Oswald Christensen, Morris Christensen, and Irven Christensen on July 16, 1927.

Approach: Hike the Garnet Canyon Trail to the Meadows (see under Central Tetons, pages 13, 16, and 17), cross the stream on a stone walkway and hike the South Fork of Garnet Canyon (no distinct trail) to the saddle between the Middle and South Tetons (11,360+ feet).

The Route

Hike northeast (just right of the ridge crest) and gain the obvious gully that leads up and right toward the summit. Climb the gully to within 100 feet of the top, then move left a bit and scramble to the north summit. You can avoid stretches of snow by working up the rock on either side of the couloir. Allow about 5 hours to reach the summit from the Meadows in Garnet Canyon (7 or 8 hours from Lupine Meadows).

Rack: An ice axe and mountain boots are recommended as there may be some snow even in late season.

Grand Teton

A citadel of naked rock, steep ice gullies, and hanging snowfields, the Grand Teton towers 7,000 feet above the valley of Jackson Hole and is in both image and elevation (13,770 feet) the greatest peak of the range. Looking southwest from Jenny Lake, it is eclipsed by Teewinot Mountain, but from most other locations in Jackson Hole it is visible and quite striking. The Grand Teton stands as the centerpiece in two famous views: From the east in Jackson Hole it is the northernmost summit of Les Trois Tetons along with the Middle and South Tetons; from the northeast it is framed in the Cathedral Group with Teewinot and Mount Owen, which rise together in jagged relief above Cascade Canyon.

The broad assortment of excellent routes and the relatively uncomplicated approach by trail (at least from the south and east sides) make the Grand Teton an irresistible objective for climbers. It is, not surprisingly, the most popular of the Teton summits. The Grand Teton has among its alpine masterpieces such timeless trade routes as the *Owen-Spalding* and *Exum Ridge* and the long,

The Grand Teton and Mount Owen from the Southeast

Exum guides and clients on the
summit ridge of the Grand Teton.
PHOTO GREG VON DOERSTEN

Summit of the Enclosure Looking Northeast

Jackson Lake

Mount Owen

Grand Teton West Face

complex alpine imperatives of the *North Ridge* and the *Black Ice Couloir.* It is not unreasonable to assert that anyone who fancies himself an alpine climber in America must sooner or later get acquainted with this outstanding mountain.

The Grand Teton has a rich and complex climbing history, the mere highlights of which are beyond the scope of this presentation; however, the first ascent of the mountain cannot be neglected. The Grand Teton's first ascent is credited to William Owen, Franklin Spalding, Frank Peterson, and John Shive, who reached the summit on August 11, 1898,

though earlier visits to the summit are claimed by two other parties. Their route, now known as the *Owen-Spalding,* is the most moderate and popular on the peak and is, with rare exception, the only route used to descend from the summit. An excellent history of early Teton climbing is found in *Mountaineering in the Tetons: The Pioneer Period 1898 to 1940* by Fritiof Fryxell. See also *A Climber's Guide to the Teton Range* by the late Leigh Ortenburger and Reynold Jackson, which gives historical data and first ascent information for all known routes in the range. Another book of interest is *CREATION OF THE TETON*

LANDSCAPE The Geologic Story of Grand Teton National Park by J.D. Love and John C. Reed Jr., 1968, which has a more recent edition.

The Lower Saddle (about 11,650 feet) is the broad col between the Middle Teton and Grand Teton and is the usual start, or at least the finish, to nearly every outing on the peak. During the summer you'll find running water, a toilet enclosure (carryout bags only), a guide hut, a ranger hut, several stone bivouac enclosures and ... people.

Northeast from the Lower Saddle, a series of gullies and low ridges lead to the Upper Saddle (about 13,160 feet), the col between the Enclosure (about 13,320 feet) and the summit

of the Grand Teton. These gullies are bounded on the left by the southwest ridge of the Enclosure and by the Exum Ridge on the right. The Enclosure is the massive west buttress of the Grand Teton, which terminates in a secondary summit where a mysterious stone enclosure was discovered in 1872, lending the name.

The Exum Ridge could be described as the true south ridge of the Grand Teton, though such a designation is not in use. It is the leftmost of three prominent ridges on the south face of the peak along with the Petzoldt Ridge and the Underhill Ridge (farthest east). Of these, only the Exum Ridge forms a continuous line to the summit. All three ridges rise above a

Middle Teton, Grand Teton, and Mount Owen from the East

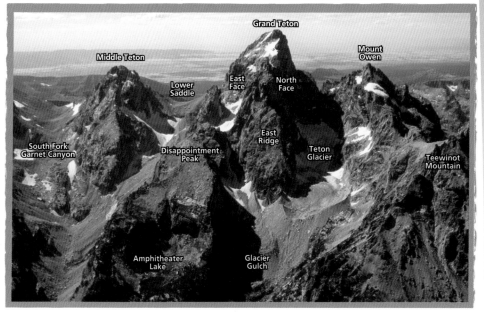

dike of black diabase that cuts across the south side of the peak from the shoulder above the Lower Saddle to the cirque north of Disappointment Peak. The Black Dike is, however, not horizontal; it runs up and down at about the 12,160-foot level like a roller coaster.

The steep east face rises above the Teepe Glacier between the Underhill Ridge and east ridge and is characterized by the Otterbody Snowfield, high on the wall. The prominent Teepe Pillar towers above the southwest side of the glacier. East of the Teepe Glacier are three pinnacles: Pemmican Pinnacle, Fairshare Tower, and the Red Sentinel. A distinct col and couloir separate these towers from the summit of Disappointment Peak (11,618 feet).

The longest continuous rampart of the peak is the east ridge, which begins between Disappointment Peak and the terminus of the Teton Glacier (about 10,400 feet), then climbs without serious interruption to the summit. The north side of the ridge drops off abruptly above the Teton Glacier to form the great north face of the Grand Teton. A broad ramp climbs 1,000 feet from the Teton Glacier to a narrow platform at the bottom of the north ridge called the Grandstand. The north ridge is formed by the junction of the upper north and west faces of the Grand Teton.

Valhalla Canyon extends northward from the Grand Teton and drops steeply into Cascade Canyon. It is bounded on the east by Mount Owen and on the west by the northwest ridge of the Grand Teton (which leads to the summit of the Enclosure). The headwall of Valhalla Canyon is formed by the rugged northwest side of the Grand Teton and the north side of the Enclosure and reaches all the way to the Upper Saddle. The west side of the Enclosure, at about the 12,000-foot level, is traversed by a long ledge system that allows passage from the Lower Saddle to routes on the northwest side of the Grand Teton and the Enclosure. This ledge is known as the Valhalla Traverse, and it brings our tour of the mountain back where it began at the Lower Saddle.

GRAND TETON—SOUTH SIDE

1. Owen-Spalding (II 5.4 to 5.6) This very popular and important route has the distinction of being the easiest route on the Grand Teton. It is the route by which the peak was first climbed and is most always the only one used to descend from the summit. The *Owen-Spalding* is perhaps less aesthetic than the *Exum Ridge* and other steeper routes, but it has the tactical advantages of being swift, direct, and it allows an easy escape in bad weather.

Approach: Begin from the Lupine Meadows Trailhead and hike the Garnet Canyon Trail and the Climbers' Trail all the way to the

Grand Teton from the Lower Saddle

Lower Saddle. The climb may be completed "car to car" in one day by an athletic team. Most folks, however, will want to make a high camp and take two or three days for the outing.

The long initial section of the *Owen-Spalding* is little more than a steep hike beginning from the Lower Saddle and following a blunt rib up the middle of a wide gully to the Upper Saddle. There are several ways to do this part of the climb, though one has become standard and requires some description.

The Route

A distinct footpath leads directly up the crest from the Lower Saddle to the Black Dike. Please use this path and avoid trampling the fragile tundra vegetation.

A prominent rib divides the gully above the Black Dike. The first steep tower along this rib is called the Needle. Follow a faint path over rocky terrain to the left (west) of the Needle and continue for several hundred feet to where a short chimney with a chockstone rises to the east. Do not climb the chimney, but continue to the north until it is possible

Grand Teton—*Owen-Spalding* Route

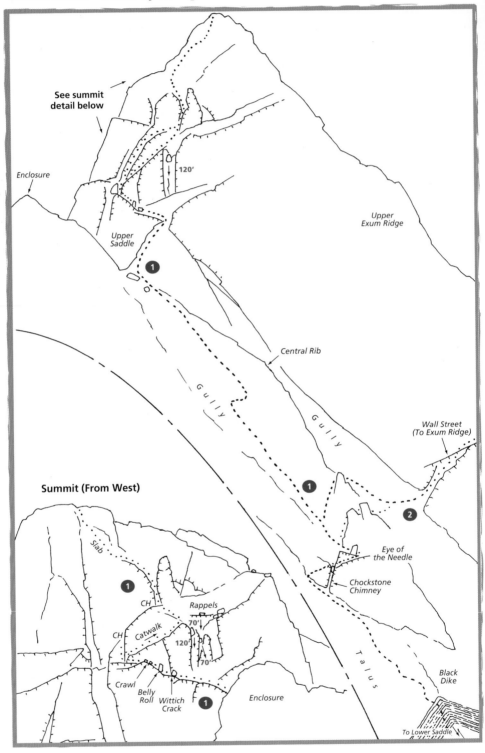

to traverse back right over the top of the chockstone and onto a wide bench with a good view to the south. Turn north and encounter a large, conspicuous boulder. Crawl through the tunnel formed by the boulder (the Eye of the Needle) and continue north along a ledge past an exposed corner (the Belly Roll Almost) to the gully above the chockstone chimney. This gully is the cutoff point for the *Exum Ridge* route.

Follow easy ledges and scree (or snow) to an area of black rock. Make a few steep moves up onto the crest of the central rib and continue just on its right side for a couple of hundred feet, then work back into the main gully and scramble for another 300 feet to the Upper Saddle. A simple alternative is to follow the right edge of the gully all the way to the Upper Saddle.

Note that from winter to early summer the entire route between the Black Dike and the Upper Saddle may be climbed on snow in the broad gully to the west of the Needle and the central rib. An ice axe, mountain boots, and crampons are usually necessary from early to mid-summer.

Work up and left from the Upper Saddle, (east then north) along a scree ledge to where it narrows over the exposed west face of the Grand Teton. Pass beneath the steep *Wittich Crack* and in about 12 feet reach the Belly Roll, a large detached slab that is passed by a hand traverse along its

upper edge. In a few more feet you encounter another obstacle known as the Crawl. Ooze through this narrow space or drop down and hand traverse along the edge, then regain the ledge and continue about 10 feet to an overhanging slot known as the Double Chimney, which is not actually double. The name refers to the chimney as it existed until the summer of 1951 when a large flake that split the chimney collapsed against its north wall.

Climb the chimney (5.5, more difficult when icy) to a rubble-strewn ledge and choose between two options: (1) Continue upward via the Owen Chimney and traverse southeast to the base of another chimney (Sargent's Chimney) that cuts east through the next cliffband; or (2) scramble up and right along the Catwalk, a sloping ramp that leads south to an overlook above the *Owen-Spalding* rappel. This rappel is normally used on the descent, and it is a good idea to verify its location at this time. From the south end of the Catwalk, scramble northeast up to the bottom of Sargent's Chimney.

Climb the left side of the chimney for about 50 feet, then branch left and continue to the top of a short dihedral. An easy, though slightly indirect, scramble leads northeast to the bottom of a 30-foot slab where a cairn can be seen on the skyline. Start up the middle of the slab, then traverse to an obvious crack on the right. Follow the crack up and left to the cairn and hike south to the summit.

Wittich Crack (5.6) is sometimes less icy than the Double Chimney and adds two pitches of excellent rock to the ascent. Begin at the obvious vertical crack system about 12 feet before reaching the Belly Roll. Climb straight up and belay in an alcove beneath an overhang. Climb out around the left side of the overhang and arrive midway along the Catwalk. This route was first climbed by Hans Wittich, Walter Becker, and Rudolph Weidner on June 27, 1931.

Rack: Light rock rack up to 2 inches.

Descent: Pay close attention to the direction of travel and notable features on the ascent, since the route must be reversed to get back to the Upper Saddle. The value of this is particularly evident during bad weather. Return to the cairn just north of the summit. Downclimb about 200 feet southwest to the top of Sargent's Chimney in the upper cliffband. Descend the chimney, then continue another 100 feet to the southwest past the Catwalk to the top of the rappel. Look for slings around a 6-foot block, about 40 feet south of the Catwalk. Rappel 120 feet to a ledge of broken rock, then scramble down to the Upper Saddle. An alternate rappel route can be done with a single rope. Begin on a ledge higher and to the southeast of the main rappel. Rappel 70 feet from slings around a block to a chockstone in a chimney. Make a second 70-foot rappel to reach the

Descending the 30-foot slab at the top of the *Owen-Spalding* route.

Rappelling off the *Owen-Spalding* route in winter.

scree ledge just south of the main rappel finish. It is also possible in dry conditions to downclimb the *Owen-Spalding* route from the summit to the Upper Saddle.

The easiest line of descent from the Upper Saddle is to reverse the standard route and go back through the Eye of the Needle. Remember to first head southwest to avoid the more difficult gully between the central rib and the Exum Ridge.

Descent alternative from the Upper Saddle: Follow the scree path down to the top right side of the central rib where the path breaks right

into steep, loose scree. Follow a discernable path along the crest of the rib for several hundred feet, pass through a gap, and descend easy ledges west to regain the standard path below the steep, loose section.

Descent alternative for the Needle: Turn right (west) about 200 feet before reaching the Chockstone Chimney and squeeze down a 15-foot slot to walking terrain on the west side of the central rib. Slings have been installed in this chimney to facilitate safe descent. This option is also useful on the ascent to pass slow parties bogged down in the Eye of the Needle and Belly Roll Almost.

2. Exum Ridge (II 5.5) This is the line of Glenn Exum's original solo ascent. The *Owen-Spalding* and the *Exum Ridge* are the two most popular routes on the Grand Teton. Whereas the *Owen-Spalding* is the easiest line to the summit, being no more than a steep hike for most of its course, the *Exum Ridge* provides more of a climbing challenge. Solid rock, interesting routefinding, and commanding position along the south ridge of the highest peak in the range combine to yield one of the classic ascents of North American climbing. Most parties ascend only the upper, more moderate section of the ridge by traversing in along a ledge called Wall Street. The lower section

Climber on the Exum Ridge (II 5.4).
PHOTO GREG VON DOERSTEN

is considerably steeper and more difficult, but if skill and experience allow,
the entire 2,500-foot ascent from the
Black Dike is highly recommended.

The Exum Ridge is easily identified from the Lower Saddle as the
serrated skyline ridge that descends
from the summit and forms the right
(east) wall of the broad gully above
and northeast of the Lower Saddle.
The upper ridge was first climbed by
Glenn Exum, who soloed the route
as the maiden voyage of his climbing
career on July 15, 1931. The entire
ridge beginning from the Black Dike
was first climbed by Jack Durrance
and Ken Henderson on September 1,
1936, and is sometimes referred to as
the *Complete Exum Ridge*.

Approach: Follow the *Owen-
Spalding* route to the steep gully
(upper chockstone chimney) just
beyond the Belly Roll Almost. Then
scramble east to the crest of the central rib or reach the crest at a gap a
short way farther north. Wall Street
is clearly visible from here as a long,
straight ledge that angles up and
right to the skyline of the ridge. Make
a descending traverse into the big
gully to the east (Wall Street Couloir)
and scramble up onto Wall Street.

The Route
Walk up the broad, diagonal ledge to
where it ends about 60 feet short of
the ridge crest. Most parties will want
to rope up here. Cross the gap, most

Exum Ridge from the Southwest

Buckingham
Buttress

Wall
Street

Petzoldt
Ridge

2

3

Black Dike

Exum Ridge

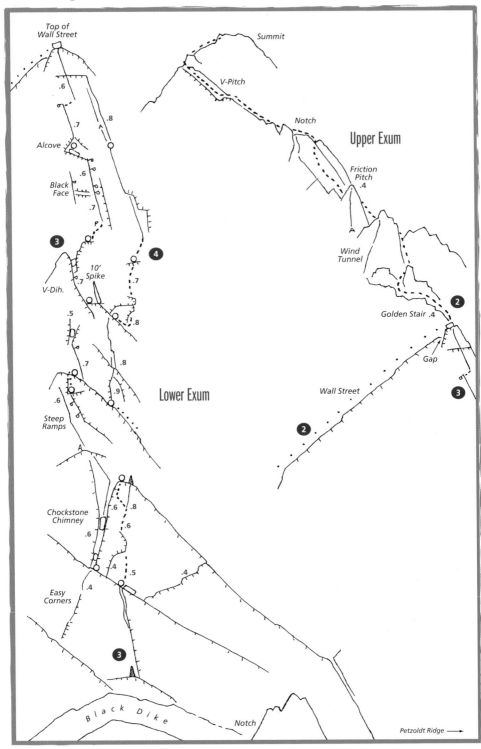

Top of Wall Street

Summit

V-Pitch

Notch

Upper Exum

.6

.7 .8

Alcove

.6

Black Face

.7

Friction Pitch .4

3

V-Dih.

10' Spike

4

.7

Wind Tunnel

.5

.7 .8

.8

Lower Exum

.9

Golden Stair .4

2

.6

Steep Ramps

Gap

Wall Street

3

A

2

Chockstone Chimney

.6 .8

.6

.6

.4 .5

.4

Easy Corners

.4

3

B l a c k   D i k e

Notch

Petzoldt Ridge ⟶

easily via hand traverse. Step down then right on some black knobs and stem to the big ledge on the prow of the ridge. You are now on the south ridge of the Grand Teton about 1,500 feet from the summit.

Climb directly up the crest on solid, knobby rock (5.4) or work around to the northeast and ascend easy cracks back to the crest. This initial 60-foot step is called the Golden Stair. Scramble about 160 feet up an almost level section to a large tower that miraculously has escaped being named. Traverse right (east) for a rope length, then go up either side of a steep gully/chimney (sometimes icy) called the Wind Tunnel for two pitches. Head up through terraces and a short chimney on the west side of the crest to reach a ledge at the base of a smooth, clean slab. You can also reach this point via a gully on the right beneath a huge left-facing dihedral.

The next rope length is known as the Friction Pitch, which is the crux of the climb and rather poorly protected. Move up and slightly left on friction to two black knobs (5.5), then go up and right to a shallow groove and upward to the top of the slab. Scramble up and right from here to a small notch that may contain snow or ice. Work northwest along the right side of the crest for about 300 feet until it is possible to move left into a prominent left-facing dihedral/ramp variously called the V, V-Pitch, or Open Book. Pass the V in 150 feet, then scramble across an easy section to the next step in the ridge. Move down a bit to the west and make an awkward lieback to pass this step. Option: From the base of the step, it is possible to make a descending traverse northwest to the top of the *Owen-Spalding* rappel as a means of escape.

Continue up to another step that is passed via a short crack, then follow the ridge crest to the base of the summit block. Traverse east about 50 feet, then angle up over broken ground to the summit.

"The Horse" provides a good alternate finish: From the base of the summit block, traverse around to the west side and climb up to a knife-edge ridge that is followed 180 feet to the summit.

Rack: Light rock rack up to 2 inches.

Descent: It is possible to reverse the route to Wall Street, but it is much easier to downclimb and rappel the *Owen-Spalding.*

3. Lower Exum Ridge (III 5.7) The *Lower Exum Ridge* is one of the great rock climbs in the Tetons. It features steep climbing on excellent rock commanding position and is fairly even in grade. The route is often climbed only to Wall Street.

Approach: From the Lower Saddle, follow the path northward through the tundra as for the *Owen-Spalding.* Break right (east) at a point short of the Black Dike and follow a

Lower Exum Ridge, Petzoldt Ridge, and Underhill Ridge as Seen from the Approach above the Lower Saddle

faint path up over a promontory, then contour to a ledge 150 feet beneath the chockstone chimney of the first pitch. From the Lower Saddle this chimney appears as a large, west-facing dihedral. Most parties will want to rope up here.

The Route

An easy initial pitch works around to the left, up easy corners and through a bulge (5.4) to reach the ledge beneath the chimney. A more difficult start takes a steep left-facing dihedral that begins at a cairn on the next ledge up. The easiest way to reach the chimney is to continue farther along the Black Dike toward the Petzoldt Ridge and follow a long, grassy ramp back left to the ledge.

Pitch 1a: Climb the large chimney past two chockstones (5.6) to reach a pedestal at the top of another long ramp (135 feet). Pitch 1b: Climb the south-facing wall to the right of the chimney and work back left near the top (5.6). The cracks that continue straight up are more difficult (5.8 or 5.9). **Pitch 2:** Follow an easy ramp up to the left, then climb a dihedral and crack to a belay just below a major step in the ridge (5.6, 150 feet). Move the belay up to the next steep section. **Pitch 3:** Jam up a hand crack to a wedged block, then work up and right to belay on a sandy ledge with a 10-foot detached flake (5.7, 100 feet). **Pitch 4:** Grunt up a V-shaped chimney with a wide crack (5.7) to a tunnel formed by a chockstone, climb out around either side (5.6), and go up a short crack to a small ledge at the base of the Black Face (65 feet). **Pitch 5:** Move up and right past a fixed pin, then follow a steep crack with more fixed pins to an alcove with a large, detached block (5.7, 110 feet). **Pitch 6:** Jam straight up a flared hand crack (5.7) to a fixed pin, traverse right, and ascend another crack to the top of Wall Street (5.7, 110 feet). It is possible (but not recommended) to avoid this pitch by working around to the left on easier terrain.

Rack: Standard rock rack up to 3 inches.

Descent: Scramble down Wall Street or continue with the *Upper Exum,* then downclimb and rappel the *Owen-Spalding* route from the summit.

4. Gold Face (III 5.10a) This four-pitch variation was first climbed by Teton rangers Renny Jackson and Jim Woodmency on June 27, 1988. It features steep climbing on excellent Teton rock a short way right of the regular route. It may be reached via a short descent east from the top of the second pitch of the *Lower Exum Ridge* or by ascending the middle of three long ramps that angle up and left from the Black Dike (see topo).

PETZOLDT RIDGE

The Petzoldt Ridge is the next large buttress to the right of the Exum Ridge. It is defined by the Beckey

Petzoldt Ridge (left) and Underhill Ridge (right)

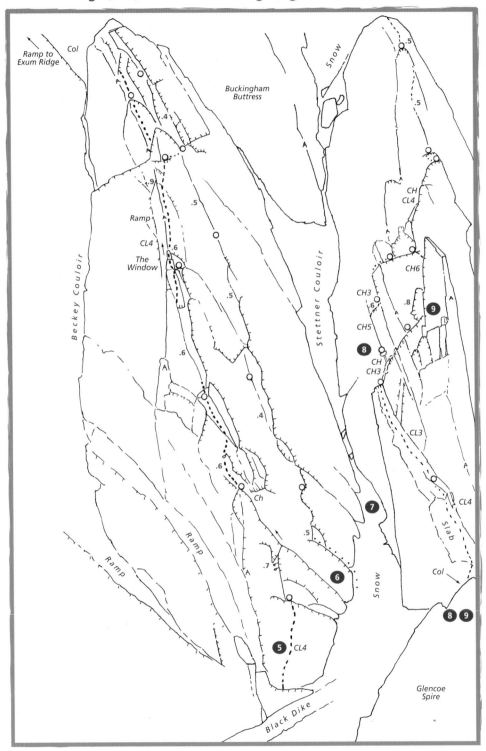

Couloir on the left and the Stettner Couloir on the right. The ridge begins from the Black Dike and ends about halfway to the summit, roughly level with the top of Wall Street. It features two classic routes on excellent rock, either of which are good alternatives to the well-traveled *Exum Ridge*.

5. Direct Petzoldt Ridge (III 5.7) This is not a variation of the original *Petzoldt Ridge,* but an independent line that follows the crest of the buttress to its top. It was first climbed by Willi Unsoeld, LaRee Munns, James Shirley, Rodney Shirley, and Austin Flint on August 30, 1953.

Approach: Follow the Black Dike as for the *Lower Exum Ridge,* but continue east to the bottom of the buttress.

The Route

Scramble directly up the ridge for about 200 feet to a good ledge, or start up the *Stettner Couloir* and traverse left onto the same ledge.

Pitch 1: Climb through a slot with some fixed pins (5.7) and gain a ramp that is followed up and left. Negotiate a short chimney and belay up to the left. **Pitch 2a:** Climb the face out and left around a black overhang (5.6) and belay at the top of a ramp/dihedral. **Pitch 2b:** Double Overhang. Move 10 feet right to the base of a big left-facing dihedral. Climb the dihedral past two difficult roofs (5.9) and join the regular route at the top

of the dihedral. This was first climbed by George Montopoli and Leo Larson on June 25, 1986. **Pitch 3:** Follow a crack system to a belay beside a tunnel in the ridge crest called the Window (5.6). **Pitch 4a:** Climb the crest of the ridge over the Window and continue up excellent rock to a belay near a pinnacle (5.6). **Pitch 4b:** Go west through the Window and follow a ramp until a short, difficult crack can be climbed back to the ridge crest (5.9). **Pitch 5:** Climb excellent rock to the right of the crest and belay on a ledge. **Pitch 6:** Climb directly up the crest and belay on a ledge. **Pitch 7:** Work up and right and gain the summit of the ridge.

Rack: Standard rack as described in the Introduction or full gear up to 3 inches.

Descent: Rappel 50 feet to the notch on the north side of the ridge and choose from the following descent options:

Petzoldt-Exum Traverse: From the notch, follow a ramp up to the west (5.6) and join the *Exum Ridge* above the Golden Stair, where you may continue to the summit or rappel 60 feet and descend Wall Street.

Ford Couloir: Climb the snow couloir between the Exum Ridge and Buckingham Buttress to the final section of the *Exum Ridge* and continue to the summit.

Buckingham Buttress: Traverse right after about 300 feet in the *Ford Couloir* and climb the upper

Buckingham Buttress to the same fate. An ice axe and perhaps crampons are needed for this finish.

6. Petzoldt Ridge (III 5.6) The *Petzoldt Ridge* route is one of the best moderate rock climbs on the Grand Teton and is an important alternative to the busy *Exum Ridge*. An ice axe will be needed through most of the summer either for the approach from the Lower Saddle or for ascending the *Ford Couloir* above the ridge. After midsummer the *Petzoldt-Exum Traverse* may allow an ascent to the summit without snow travel.

Approach: From the Lower Saddle, approach as for the *Lower Exum Ridge,* but continue east along the Black Dike into the *Stettner Couloir* along the east side of the buttress. Climb up the couloir (most likely on snow) until a ledge provides a traverse onto the face.

The Route

There are many options on this route, including the location of belays.

Pitch 1: Traverse up onto the face, climb a black chimney (5.5), then work up slabs to belay beneath an open book. **Pitch 2:** Climb a large left-facing dihedral and belay beneath a roof (5.4). **Pitch 3:** Climb through the roof, go up a short left-facing corner, and follow a crack to a belay stance (5.5, 150 feet). **Pitch 4:** Follow the crack system to belay on a ledge left of a large roof (5.5, 150 feet). **Pitch 5:** Climb a gully or

the ridge on the left and belay beneath a short chimney (5.4, 120 feet). **Pitch 6:** Climb the chimney and scramble to the top of the ridge (5.3).

Rack: Full rock gear up to 3 inches.

Descent: Rappel 50 feet to the notch on the north side of the ridge and choose from the options listed for *Direct Petzoldt Ridge* (above).

7. Stettner Couloir (III 5.7 AI3) This is the steep couloir between the Petzoldt Ridge and Underhill Ridge. It provides an excellent snow and ice route to the summit in early summer; by mid to late season, some of the snow will be gone and you will encounter rock climbing up to 5.7 in difficulty. The route was first climbed by Sam Younger and Albert Strube on July 30, 1933, apparently trying to find the *Owen-Spalding*. An ice axe and crampons are recommended along with a light rock climbing rack and a few ice screws.

Approach: Begin from the Lower Saddle as for the *Lower Exum Ridge*. Continue east along the Black Dike past the bottom of the Petzoldt Ridge and head up into the couloir.

The Route

Follow the narrow couloir to where it branches beneath the Buckingham Buttress. The left fork leads over slabs to the col just north of the Petzoldt Ridge, where you could finish with the *Ford Couloir* (see above). The right branch goes straight up a steep, narrow ice couloir to the col above the Underhill Ridge. Climb a short rock pitch (5.6) above the col to get up onto the broad southeast face. Climb snow or the Buckingham Buttress on the left and finish as for the *Exum Ridge*. An alternate finish can be made up either of two large chimneys at the top of the southeast face (5.4).

Rack: Full rock gear up to 3 inches.

Descent: Downclimb and rappel the *Owen-Spalding* from the summit. If the left branch of the couloir is taken it is simple enough to climb the Petzoldt-Exum Traverse and descend Wall Street.

UNDERHILL RIDGE

The Underhill Ridge is the large buttress to the east of the Petzoldt Ridge. It is defined by the Stettner Couloir on the left, but merges on the right with a large southeast-facing wall called the East Face of the Grand Teton. There is a shallow col behind the top of the Underhill Ridge, beyond which the southeast snowfields reach up to the summit. The curiously shaped Otterbody Snowfield is just north from the col and helps identify the ridge from the east. The Underhill Ridge appears on the right skyline from the Lower Saddle.

8. Underhill Ridge (III 5.6) This route generally ascends the crest of the ridge, but passes the more difficult middle section on the west side. It was first climbed by Robert Underhill, Phil Smith, and Francis Truslow on July 15, 1931.

Approach: Begin from the Lower Saddle as for the *Lower Exum Ridge* and follow the Black Dike to its high point at the Glencoe Col (the notch between Glencoe Spire and the Underhill Ridge).

The Route

Scramble north from the col across the bottom of a large slab to the base of a prominent tower. Follow cracks up the slab for 130 feet (Class 4) and continue in a westerly direction to the top of a long ramp (Class 3). Scramble up broken ledges on the west side of the ridge to the bottom of a short chimney.

Pitch 1: Climb the chimney to a broad ledge (Class 4). The difficult Underhill chimney begins from this ledge. **Pitch 2:** Do not climb the chimney, but work around the corner to the left and climb an easier chimney until a bulge impedes upward progress. Make difficult moves right to a tiny ledge, then pull up and right (5.6, no pro) into the first (Underhill) chimney and belay. **Pitch 3:** Climb the chimney for about 60 feet and belay on a ledge (5.4). **Pitch 4:** A long pitch up a chimney/dihedral leads to a ledge on the crest of the ridge (Class 4). **Pitch 5:** Follow a crack up the middle of the narrow face and belay on a ledge near the top (5.5).

Pitch 6: Climb a final short step (5.5) and follow easy rock to the top of the ridge. The last two pitches can be combined.

Cross the col and climb snow or easy rock to a steeper section. A short pitch (5.6) leads to the southeast snowfield, which is followed to the summit block. Climb either of two moderate chimneys (5.4) or finish to the left as for *Exum Ridge.*

Rack: An ice axe is recommended for ascents of this ridge at least until late summer. Bring rock gear up to 3 inches.

Descent: Downclimb and rappel the *Owen-Spalding.*

9. Direct Underhill Ridge (III 5.8)

This difficult variation stays more on the crest of the ridge and avoids the often wet chimneys of the regular route. From the Lower Saddle a conspicuous tower of white rock can be seen on the skyline of the Underhill Ridge. The route climbs the chimney between the white tower and the main buttress instead of traversing around onto the west side, then rejoins the original line after two pitches. It was first climbed by William Buckingham, Steve Smale, Ann Blackenburg, Charles Browning, and Jack Hilberry on August 30, 1953.

The Route

Climb the initial slab and ramp of the regular route to where the ledge system goes around onto the west side. Scramble up and right on broken black rock to the bottom of the chimney that separates the white tower from the main ridge. **Pitch 1:** Climb a corner on the left that at first overhangs, then becomes vertical (5.8). Climb to the top of the chimney, then traverse right into the chimney. It is also possible to climb a good crack in the face on the left (5.9). Climb the chimney past some chockstones to the notch between the tower and the main ridge and belay (5.6). **Pitch 2:** Climb up and left and join the regular route as shown in the topo.

Rack: An ice axe is recommended for ascents of this ridge at least until late summer. Bring rock gear up to 3 inches.

Descent: Downclimb and rappel the *Owen-Spalding* route from the summit.

EAST RIDGE

The east ridge is the longest continuous feature of the Grand Teton. It begins from the south side of the terminal moraine of the Teton Glacier (about 10,400 feet) and climbs without significant interruption to the summit.

10. East Ridge (III 5.7)

The ascent of this ridge would be straightforward and relatively easy but for two large towers, the Molar Tooth and the Second Tower, both of which require a tricky and obscure bypass. The ridge

East Ridge of the Grand Teton

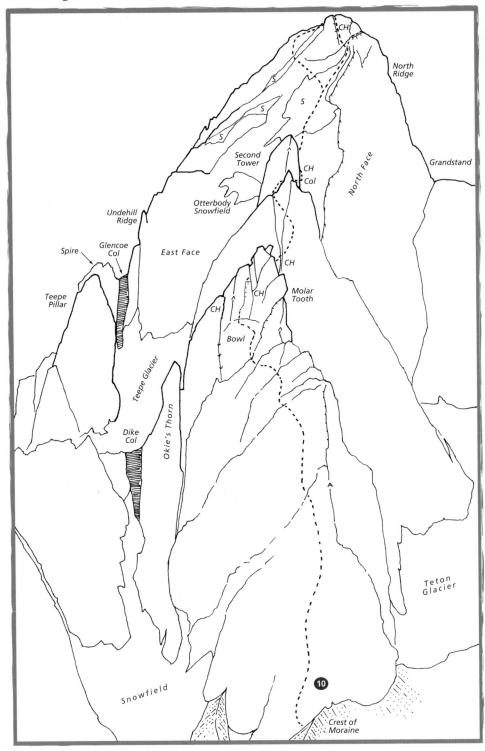

East Ridge from the Summit Block in Late August

Disappointment
Peak

Glacier
Gulch

Second
Tower

Garnet
Canyon

Molar
Tooth

was attempted repeatedly before its first successful ascent by Robert Underhill and Kenneth Henderson on July 22, 1929. This was the first new route on the Grand Teton since the completion of the *Owen-Spalding* in 1898. The *East Ridge* is a long and varied alpine route that should not be underestimated.

Approach: See the description for the Amphitheater Lake Trail (aka Glacier Trail) on page 14. Hike up onto the terminal moraine of the Teton Glacier and proceed to its southern extreme. The route begins about 50 feet south from the crest of the moraine.

The Route

Scramble up the broad ridge, keeping left of the crest for about 2,000 feet to a large bowl beneath the Molar Tooth. The original route passed this formidable tower by an intricate traverse along its north side. The standard method now is to climb around or over its south side. Two chimneys can be seen rising on the left above a bowl. The route takes the more broken chimney on the left; however, the rock just to its left can be climbed for one pitch before the chimney is entered. Cut right at a ledge and continue in the upper chimney to a notch called the Window. The Teepe

Glacier can be seen below to the south. There are two ways to proceed from the Window. **Option 1:** Descend a steep scree gully into the large couloir that rises from the Teepe Glacier, then climb the couloir on snow or ice to the giant chockstone at its top. Pass the chockstone on the right and continue on snow or rock for another 75 feet to the notch above the Molar Tooth. **Option 2:** Tricky traverse. From a ledge west of the window, climb an obvious crack (5.7) that leads up and left around a corner to a ramp. Climb a wide crack (5.7) from the north end of the ramp to a ledge that angles up to the left. Traverse a steep face through an area of broken rock to the crest of a ridge. Traverse snow or scree to the top of the giant chockstone and continue up into the notch west of the Molar Tooth.

Climb a short, difficult pitch to get out of the notch above the Molar Tooth (5.7), then work up and right and climb an easy chimney that leads to an alcove. Climb right out of the alcove and follow slabs for a couple of pitches, then angle up and left along ledges for several hundred feet to gain the crest of a spur that descends to the south from a pinnacle on the ridge crest. Scramble around to the west side of this spur and climb a gully (snow-filled in early season) to the notch between the pinnacle and the summit of the Second Tower (on the west). The Second Tower now can be passed via ledges

on its north side. About halfway across, downclimb about 10 feet and pass behind a large flake, then climb a short chimney and continue on easier ground to the large platform at the west side of the Second Tower.

Climb steep scree or snow-covered slabs and gain the east snowfield. There are several ways to reach the summit from the *East Ridge* snowfield. **Option 1:** Climb directly to the summit block on snow or (in late season) climb rock to the right along the edge of the north face. At the top of the snowfield, climb a steep, open chimney to the summit (5.6). **Option 2:** Climb way around to the left on snow and finish as for the *Exum Ridge*. **Option 3:** Work around to the north side of the summit block and climb a chimney that leads to the *North Ridge* route 100 feet below the the summit. **Option 4:** Follow a diagonal ledge system above the north face to the top of the "V" gully (see *North Face,* below) where an awkward chimney leads to the final blocks and the summit.

Rack: An ice axe, crampons, and light rock gear up to 3 inches.

Descent: Downclimb and rappel the *Owen-Spalding* from the summit.

GRAND TETON—NORTH FACE

11. North Face (IV 5.6 or 5.8) No collection of the best climbs in the Tetons would be complete without the *North Face* of the Grand Teton. Steeped in shadow on the cold side

Second
Tower

10

12   Grandstand

11

Teton Glacier

Grand Teton—North Face

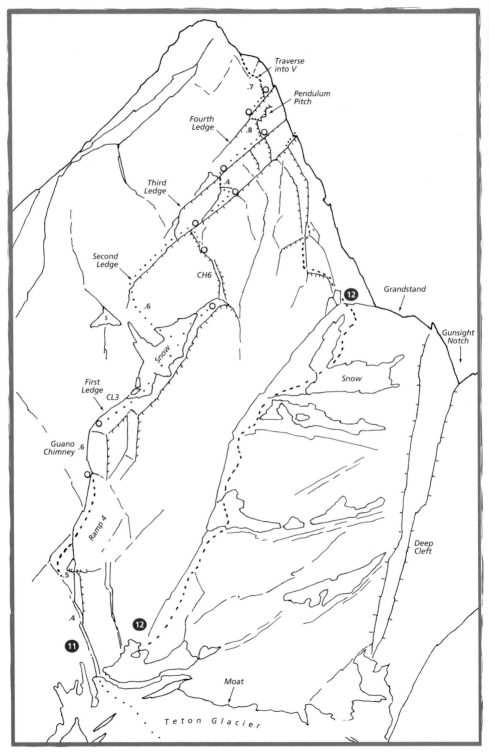

of the mountain, this complex mixed route is one of the great alpine challenges of the range. The face was first climbed on August 25, 1936, by Paul Petzoldt, Eldon Petzoldt, and Jack Durrance, who climbed to the Third Ledge then rappelled back to the Second Ledge and traversed around to finish via the *North Ridge*. Their ascent was made from Jenny Lake in a single day. The *North Face Direct Finish* or *Direct North Face,* which is now the standard line, ascends the very steep upper wall to the left of the *North Ridge* and was pieced together by different parties between 1941 and 1953. The entire route, including the first free ascent of the Pendulum Pitch and the final traverse into the "V," was completed by Richard Emerson, Willi Unsoeld, and Leigh Ortenburger on July 24, 1953. The face is about 2,500 feet high, tends to hold snow and ice on ledges, and has considerable hazard from rockfall on the initial pitches. Intelligent planning and speed of ascent are of the essence!

Approach: See the description for the Amphitheater Lake Trail (aka Glacier Trail) under Trails, Central Tetons. Hike in via the Glacier Trail and climb to the top left corner of the Teton Glacier. Take precautions for crevasses.

The Route

From the upper part of the Teton Glacier, note two deep chimneys left from the bottom of the Grandstand. Cross the moat (and/or bergschrund as needed), then move up and left onto a ledge system at the base of the left chimney. The right (more westerly) chimney is loose and dangerous. It may be possible to avoid most of the glacier and the moat crossing by ascending a long, diagonal ledge up to the base of the left chimney. Ascend the chimney for several moderate pitches, then move up and right along a ledge system to Guano Chimney, a deep cleft that leads to the First Ledge. Climb the chimney to First Ledge (5.6), where a bivouac can be made in a cave about 100 feet from the top of the chimney.

Scramble all the way to the west end of the First Ledge. Climb a steep, shallow chimney for about 130 feet (5.6) and belay. Then work up and left on friction to reach the Second Ledge. Scramble up to the right for 300 feet until an obvious break leads directly up to the Third Ledge. Scramble another 300 feet or so up the Third Ledge to a right-facing dihedral just short of some rappel slings. This is the start to the Pendulum Pitch and is also a good place to exit the face in the event of running late, bad weather, or to follow the line of the original 1936 ascent. To escape, rappel 120 feet to the Second Ledge, traverse up and westward to intersect the *North Ridge* route, then traverse the west face to the Upper Saddle.

To continue up the Pendulum Pitch, ascend the dihedral for about

60 feet (5.7), then work left on a sloping, tapering ledge and make a blind traverse left (5.8). Climb up into a black alcove at the east end of the Fourth Ledge. Move the belay about 100 feet up the ledge to start the last difficult pitch (this is only about 50 feet from the north ridge). Move back left (east) to a small right-facing dihedral and climb to its top. Traverse up and left on friction (5.7) for about 35 feet to reach the "V," a large recess in the upper north face from which a scramble of several hundred feet leads to the summit.

Variation (5.6): The Second Ledge may also be reached from its east end. Climb to the upper left extreme of the snowfield on the First Ledge, then continue up broken rock to the east end of the Second Ledge.

This was first climbed by Paul Petzoldt, Bernice Petzoldt, Glen Exum, and Hans Kraus on August 14, 1941.

Rack: Ice axe, crampons, and a full rock rack up to 3 inches.

Descent: Downclimb and rappel the *Owen-Spalding* route from the summit.

12. North Ridge (IV 5.8) The *North Ridge* of the Grand Teton is a long and complex alpine climb, probably the most difficult route in North America at the time of its first ascent. It has withstood the test of time and is still considered a serious undertaking by experienced alpine climbers. The route begins atop the Grandstand and ascends a series of ledges and chimneys to finish on the right side of the ridge crest above Second Ledge.

Climbing the *North Ridge* of the Grand Teton (IV 5.8).
PHOTO GREG VON DOERSTON

Grand Teton from the Northwest

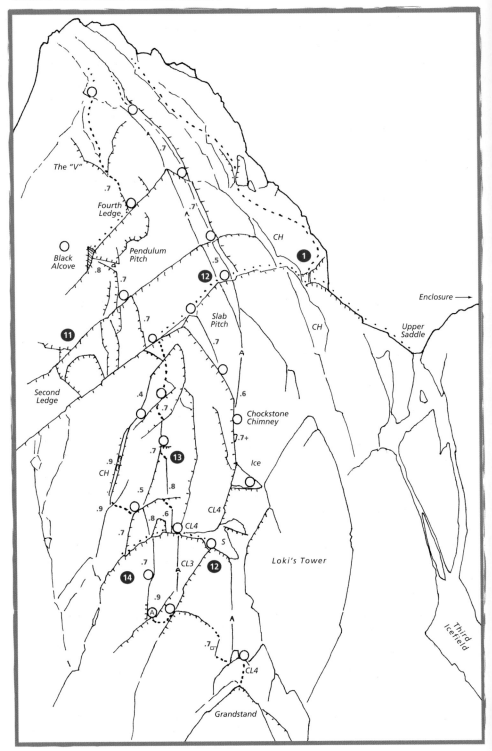

It is also possible to finish as for the *Direct North Face,* which adds notably to the overall difficulty of the ascent. Robert Underhill and Fritiof Fryxell made the first ascent on July 19, 1931.

Approach: The Grandstand, from which the route proceeds, may be approached from the east via the Teton Glacier or from the west via Valhalla Canyon, the latter of which has become more popular.

East Side Approach: See the description for the Amphitheater Lake Trail (aka Glacier Trail) on page 14. From Amphitheater Lake, follow the climber's path north over a ridge and down into Glacier Gulch. Pass beneath the east ridge of the Grand Teton, go up over the moraine, and climb the Teton Glacier to its upper southwest corner. Cross the moat and gain the east wall of the Grandstand. Just crossing the moat can be an ordeal. The easiest line is typically along its left side, but it's no piece of cake. Expect some rockfall from the north face and tricky routefinding on steep snow and wet slabs.

West Side Approach: The west side of the Grandstand is reached from Valhalla Canyon via Cascade Canyon or the Valhalla Traverse. The best stragegy is to make a very early start from the Lower Saddle and take the Valhalla Traverse (see above) around to the ice bowl on the north side of the Enclosure. Follow a steep, exposed ramp down to the second icefield of the *Black Ice Couloir,* then make an ascending traverse to the lower of three large ramps that diagonals up across the northwest face of the Grand Teton. Expect wet slabs, snow, ice, or all the above along this ramp; however, much of this can be avoided in late season by staying as far left as possible. The ramp is a scramble in dry conditions and is contiguous with the west side of the Grandstand, where a reasonable scramble leads out left then back right to the top.

The Route
From the top of the Grandstand, scramble up beside a large block and belay. **Pitch 1:** Go left behind the block, then work up past some old fixed pins (5.7) and left to a ledge that is followed into a gully. **Pitch 2:** Scramble up the gully and belay on a bench (Class 3). **Pitch 3:** Climb a short, steep wall of dark rock (5.7) and continue to a shelf (usually snow-covered) at the base of the notorious Chockstone Chimney. **Pitch 4:** Climb directly up the steep chimney, then stem up and pass the chockstone on the left (5.7 to 5.9 depending on who tells the story) and belay just above. **Pitch 5:** Continue up the chimney and belay at its top (5.7). **Pitch 6:** Climb a steep slab with poor protection, first going up and left to the arête (5.6 to 5.7) then back right to arrive at the Second Ledge of the *North Face.* This pitch is very difficult if iced up and may require crampons. **Pitch 7:**

Traverse up and right along the ledge to the west side of the ridge, which at this point could be described as the northwest arête of the Grand Teton. **Pitch 8:** Climb up to the Third Ledge of the *North Face* route and belay. **Pitch 9:** Follow a left-facing corner and chimney system to the Fourth Ledge of the *North Face* and belay (5.7). **Pitch 10:** Continue in the same system for another pitch (5.7), then scramble 400 feet to the summit.

For a more rapid ascent from the Second Ledge (top of pitch 5), it is possible to traverse right almost to the Great West Chimney and scramble to the summit. This is the easiest finish to the *North Ridge*. The *North Face Direct Finish* takes the Pendulum Pitch and the V to the summit. To escape the route from the Second Ledge, continue all the way across the west face to the Crawl on the *Owen-Spalding* and descend to the Lower Saddle.

Rack: Ice axe, crampons, mountain boots, and full rock gear. Under rare late-season conditions, the entire route from Valhalla Canyon is dry, free of snow, and can be done as a pure rock climb. Consult the Jenny Lake rangers regarding route conditions.

Descent: Downclimb and rappel the *Owen-Spalding* route.

13. Italian Cracks Variation (IV 5.8)
This is an excellent alternative to the difficult and often icy chimney and slab pitches of the regular *North Ridge*

route. The line follows a fairly direct series of cracks on the north face, out left from the immense dihedral of the Chockstone Chimney. Howard Friedman and Peter Woolen made the first ascent on August 19, 1971. They named the route in reference to George Montopoli, who was at the time away in the Peace Corps. Montopoli and Ralph Baldwin linked the *Italian Cracks* and the *North Face Direct Finish* in 1976, creating one of the great lines on the Grand Teton.

The Route
Climb the first two pitches of the standard *North Ridge* route to the big ledge, then move the belay left (east) to an obvious crack. **Pitch 3:** Climb the wide crack for about 20 feet, then traverse 15 feet left into a long, open chimney. Climb to the top of the chimney and belay on a ledge (5.7, 150 feet). It also is possible to climb straight up from the ledge (5.8) and merge left nearer to the roof. **Pitch 4:** Work up and around the left side of the roof and belay after 120 feet (5.7). **Pitch 5:** Moderate face climbing leads to the Second Ledge (5.5, 75 feet). Traverse right on the Second Ledge and finish with the standard *North Ridge*. It is, however, possible to continue up the north face as described under the *American Cracks* route.

14. American Cracks (IV 5.9) This
steep and difficult variation lies to the left of the *Italian Cracks* and poses

another alternative to the standard *North Ridge* route. It was first climbed by Mike Colacino and Calvin Hebert on July 7, 1988.

The Route
Pitch 1: Climb the first pitch of the standard *North Ridge* (5.7) and belay in the gully. **Pitch 2:** Drop down and left about 10 feet and traverse left along a ledge (Class 4) to belay on a ramp that angles up to the right. **Pitch 3:** Climb a short right-facing dihedral below a hanging flake (5.8) followed by a wide hand crack (5.9) and belay at a good stance after 75 feet. **Pitch 4:** Continue up the hand crack and belay on a good ledge with a huge block (5.7, 90 feet). The *Italian Cracks* route begins from this ledge a short way to the right. **Pitch 5:** From the big block, move down and left about 15 feet and climb a left-facing dihedral to the next ledge (5.7). This ledge can also be reached by a crack just left of the big block (5.8). **Pitch 6:** Move up and left and climb a long chimney that leans to the right. The crux is in passing some chockstones about halfway up the chimney (5.9). Belay on a ramp up and right from the end of the chimney. **Pitch 7:** Climb an easy crack up and right, then cut back left to Second Ledge (5.4). Finish as for the *North Ridge.*

North Face Direct Finish Variation
tion (IV 5.8) The direct finish to the *North Face* route adds three pitches of steep climbing to the *North Ridge* or the *Italian Cracks*. This challenging combination was first completed from the standard *North Ridge* by Jim Donini, Rick Black, and Michael Cole on August 11, 1976. It was climbed from the *Italian Cracks* by George Montopoli and Ralph Baldwin that same summer.

Look east down the Second Ledge from the standard route and locate a black chimney between two right-facing dihedrals. Climb the black chimney (5.7) to the Third Ledge of the *North Face,* then move the belay about 20 feet down to the east to the bottom of a right-facing dihedral. This is the Pendulum Pitch. Proceed as described above for the *North Face Direct Finish.*

GRAND TETON, NORTHWEST SIDE
15. Black Ice Couloir (IV 5.7, AI3+) The *Black Ice Couloir* is the most famous alpine ice climb in the Tetons and was the first major route of its kind to be established in the range. It was first climbed by Raymond Jacquot and Herb Swedlund on July 29, 1961, after at least two earlier attempts. Yvon Chouinard, Ken Weeks, and Frank Ganeau began from the First Icefield on July 7, 1958, and were turned back by falling rock and ice. Fred Beckey and Charles Bell made an unsuccessful attempt on June 26, 1961.

Central Tetons from the Northwest

Teewinot Mountain

Mount Owen

Grand Teton

Middle Teton

South Teton

Dartmouth Basin

Valhalla Canyon

South Fork Cascade Canyon

Cascade Canyon

The route is long and involved, hidden in the depths of the remote cleft between the west face of the Grand Teton and the north buttress of the Enclosure. There are three distinct icefields separated by sections of rock and a final, narrow chute that leads to the Upper Saddle. The couloir is difficult to reach by any approach, and once on the ice the only escape is up. There is some danger of rockfall from climbers on the *Owen-Spalding* route, especially during midseason. The *Black Ice Couloir* requires mastery in routefinding and the ability to move quickly over mixed terrain with full alpine gear.

Approach: There are several logistical options that depend upon path of approach and whether one plans a retrievable high camp, a carryover, or a one-day ascent. The most direct approach with the least hiking is via Valhalla Canyon. The *Black Ice Couloir* begins from the head of this canyon and climbs for about 3,000 feet to the Upper Saddle. Overnight gear must be carried up the route if camp is made in the canyon. Thus, a one-day blitz may be preferable with this approach. The only reasonable descent is via the *Owen-Spalding*. It is possible to retrieve a camp in Valhalla Canyon by taking the Valhalla Traverse back around from

Grand Teton from the Northwest, August, 1990

Grand Teton—Northwest Side

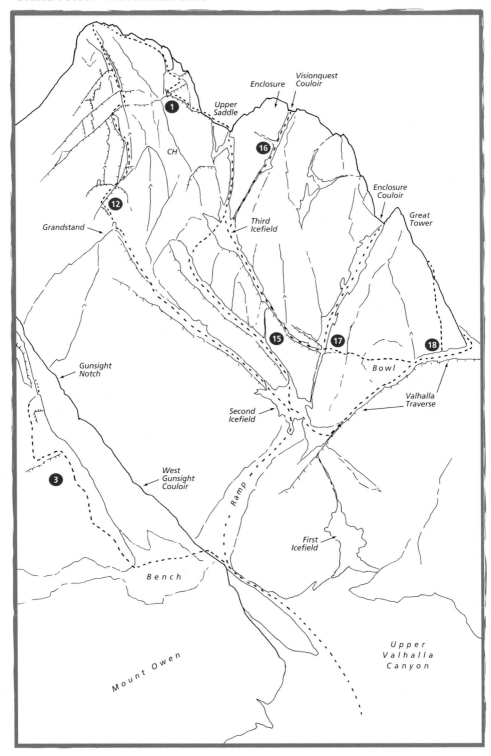

the Lower Saddle, but this is a long haul and not recommended.

The best alternative is to camp at the Lower Saddle. Take the Valhalla Traverse around to the north side of the Enclosure. Cimb the *Black Ice Couloir* to the Upper Saddle, descend the *Owen-Spalding,* and return to camp.

The Route

The route from the Lower Saddle: Start early and follow the Valhalla Traverse around to the northwest ridge of the Enclosure. Contour around to the north on a ledge that leads down to a small basin or bowl. Cross the bowl on snow or ice and follow a marginal ledge system around a buttress to the *Enclosure Ice Couloir.* Cross the couloir and ascend the lower of two diagonal ledges that traverse the north buttress of the Enclosure. Gain a long diagonal ramp that leads to the Third Icefield of the *Black Ice Couloir.* This is the higher of three long ramps that angle up and left across the lower northwest face of the Grand Teton. The Third Icefield is a continuation of the third ramp. Follow the west margin of the ice for several pitches (5.7, AI3) and belay from pitons or ice screws along the north wall of the Enclosure.

The couloir closes into a steep, narrow chute above the Third Icefield that is the crux of the route. The ice reaches an angle of 70 degrees about 120 feet up into the chute, beyond which a belay niche is found on the right. Ice screws are required for this belay. One last and easier pitch leads to the Upper Saddle. There are seven or eight pitches of ice from the bottom of the Third Icefield to the Upper Saddle, some of which may be snow-covered in early season. Be continuously alert for rockfall.

The route from Valhalla Canyon: It is possible to climb directly into the *Black Ice Couloir* from the upper reaches of Valhalla Canyon. This is the line that was attempted by Yvon Chouinard in 1958. Climb straight up through the first two icefields, then angle right into the *Enclosure Ice Couloir* and proceed as described above. This may have the appeal of climbing "the whole thing," but it also exposes the climber to the maximum hazard from rockfall. It is also worth considering that there is almost nothing left of the First Icefield (see aerial photo taken in 1990, page 61). The wiser choice is to follow the line of the first ascent.

The original route: Hike to the top of Valhalla Canyon, then go left into the *West Gunsight Couloir* and gain a ramp that leads up and right into the Second Icefield of the *Black Ice Couloir.* The *Enclosure Ice Couloir* lies straight ahead to the southwest and is accessible from the Second Icefield as is the upper ramp to the Third Icefield. Climb to the top of the Second Icefield and gain the middle ramp, which may begin with a narrow ice runnel. Climb the ramp over water-ice and smooth slabs about 500 feet to an area of black rock. Traverse up and right on broken rock and snow ledges for two pitches and arrive at the broad apron of the Third Icefield. Climb up and right across the icefield and enter the narrow chute that is the crux and final section of the climb. Finish as described above.

Rack: Ice screws, possibly pitons, and a rock rack up to 2 inches.

Descent: Descend the *Owen-Spalding* to the Lower Saddle.

16. Visionquest Couloir (IV 5.8 AI3+) This steep and sensational ice climb ascends a narrow couloir that branches west from the Third Icefield of the *Black Ice Couloir* and tops out near the summit of the Enclosure. It was first climbed by Michael Stern and Stephen Quinlan on August 10, 1981.

The Route

Climb the *Black Ice Couloir* to near the top of the Third Icefield where the *Visionquest Couloir* is visible on the right. The route begins with 40 feet of ice runnels and rock (5.8) followed by 60-degree ice in a narrow section of the couloir. The gully widens and the angle eases slightly after the first two pitches. Two more pitches of ice lead to a large chockstone that is passed on the right. Follow the upper couloir as it curves around to the top of the *Northwest Ridge* route.

Richard Rossiter approaching the Second Icefield of the *Black Ice Couloir*. The *Enclosure Ice Couloir* is straight ahead.
Photo Jeff Splittgerber

Rack: Ice screws, possibly pitons, and a rock rack up to 2 inches.

Descent: Descend the *Owen-Spalding* to the Lower Saddle.

17. Enclosure Ice Couloir (IV 5.7 AI3) The *Enclosure Ice Couloir* slashes up and right across the north face of the Enclosure to the col between the Great Tower and the final stretch of the *Northwest Ridge*. It is less steep and less subject to rockfall than the *Black Ice Couloir* and is one of the most popular alpine ice climbs in the range. Peter Lev, William Read, and

James Greig made the first ascent on July 22, 1962.

Approach: It is possible to begin the climb from the Second Icefield of the *Black Ice Couloir,* but this necessitates an approach from Valhalla Canyon or a descent to the icefield from the Valhalla Traverse. The more pleasant and logical option is to follow the Valhalla Traverse to its end at the *Enclosure Ice Couloir* about 200 feet above the Second Icefield (see *Black Ice Couloir* above).

The Route

Climb 50-degree snow or ice (depending on the season) for about 800 feet to the col between the Great Tower and the final section of the *Northwest Ridge,* which can be ascended to the summit of the Enclosure and the Upper Saddle. From here one can climb the Owen-Spalding route to the summit or just downclimb the Owen-Spalding to the Lower Saddle.

Rack: Bring typical gear for snow and ice climbing plus a light rock rack up to 2.5 inches.

Descent: Downclimb the *Owen-Spalding* route to the Lower Saddle. It is also possible to rappel and downclimb the west face of the Enclosure to the Valhalla Traverse: Descend a ledge system a good way to the south and make two long rappels from slings. Downclimb steep, loose terrain to the Valhalla Traverse ledge and follow it south to the Lower Saddle.

18. Northwest Ridge (III 5.7) The *Northwest Ridge* climbed from Cascade Canyon is the longest route on the Grand Teton. Only the section above the Valhalla Traverse is described here because it is an excellent rock climb and because its upper half is the logical conclusion to the *Enclosure Ice Couloir.* The long, lower part of the ridge is rarely climbed. Note that this ridge does not lead to the summit of the Grand Teton but to the summit of the Enclosure. Jack

Richard Rossiter at the crux of the *Black Ice Couloir* (IV 5.7 AI3+), 1976.
Photo Jeff Splittgerber

Grand Teton from the Southwest

Durrance and Michael Davis climbed the entire ridge from Cascade Canyon on August 8–10, 1938.

Approach: Hike the Garnet Canyon and Climbers' Trail to the Lower Saddle and take the Valhalla Traverse all the way around to the base of the *Northwest Ridge* (see Valhalla Traverse under Central Tetons, page 14).

The Route

Identify a good crack just south from the northwest corner of the ridge. **Pitch 1:** Climb the crack (difficult for the first 25 feet), then continue up easier corners to a belay in a band of black rock. An intermediate belay can

be made on this long pitch. **Pitches 2–6:** Traverse right over good rock around the right side of the Great Tower, staying as high as possible, to a gully that leads up toward the ridge crest. Climb to the top of the gully, then go right and up a short chimney. Continue around the south side of the ridge to a slot that leads up to the col at the top of the *Enclosure Ice Couloir*. The tradition at this point is to traverse back west along the crest of the ridge and gain the summit of the Great Tower on its south side. Some ingenuity may be required to get back down from the monolithic summit block. Cross the col to the east

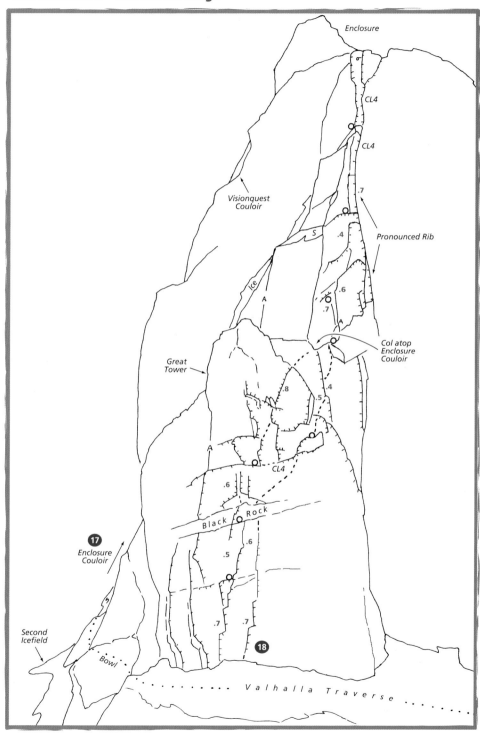

Enclosure

CL4

CL4

.7

Visionquest
Couloir

S

.4

Pronounced Rib

Ice

A

.6

.7

A

Col atop
Enclosure
Couloir

Great
Tower

.8

.4

.5

A

CL4

.6

Black Rock

.5

.6

17

Enclosure
Couloir

.5

.7

.7

18

Second
Icefield

Bowl

Valhalla Traverse

and belay beneath the next steep step in the ridge (the Second Tower). **Pitch 7:** Climb a steep crack (left of the arête of the buttress) that angles up and left to a belay beneath a roof (5.7). **Pitch 8:** Work around the right end of the roof (5.6), climb a short wall, and belay. Move the belay to the top of the tower. **Pitch 9:** Climb a crack on the right past a roof, then scramble over black rock and belay on the left (5.7). **Pitch 10:** Scramble up to a steep yellow wall and finish with an aid move at a fixed pin. The final wall can be avoided via a talus gully of black rock to the left. Scramble 150 feet northeast to reach the summit of the Enclosure.

Rack: Standard rock rack up to 3 inches.

Descent: Scramble down to the Upper Saddle and descend the *Owen-Spalding* to the Lower Saddle.

Variation: Kimbrough-Olson Crack Variation (IV 5.8) This five-pitch variation to the original route was first climbed by Tom Kimbrough and Jim Olson on July 21, 1976. It is shown at the left of the two lines indicated on the drawn topo. Begin just left of the dihedral, a short way left of the regular start. **Pitch 1:** Climb the dihedral (5.7) to a stance on the right. **Pitch 2:** Climb up and left into a band of black rock (5.6) and belay on a good ledge that extends out to the right. **Pitch 3:** Climb black rock through a break in the wall and belay on the next good ledge (5.6). **Pitches 4 and 5:** Climb an off-width crack along the edge of a flake, go up past some corners, and finish with a narrow chimney that leads up and left to easier terrain. Scramble 300 feet to a shallow gully that angles up to the left. Join the regular route to the right or jam a hand crack followed by an off-width and go right to the ridge crest.

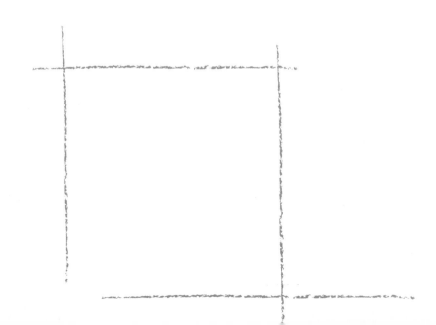

Disappointment Peak

It could be said that Disappointment Peak lives up to its name. This stumpy wedge of rock, with the loftiest peaks of the range towering above to the west, attracts little attention from tourists and mountaineers. This is not to say that the view from the summit is dreary; the view is decidedly spectacular, and the ascent from Amphitheater Lake is a splendid alpine scramble—the same scramble, in fact, made by Phil Smith and Walter Harvey, who inadvertently bagged the first ascent of Disappointment Peak on a thwarted attempt to climb the Grand Teton on August 20, 1925. In another, flatter place, the peak itself might be a national park, but virtually hidden against the backdrop of the mighty Central Tetons, it goes almost completely unnoticed . . . except by rock climbers.

Disappointment Peak is situated immediately southeast of the Grand Teton and forms the divide between Glacier Gulch and Garnet Canyon. It has a very steep, 1,000-foot north face that has seen some climbing

Disappointment Peak from the Southeast

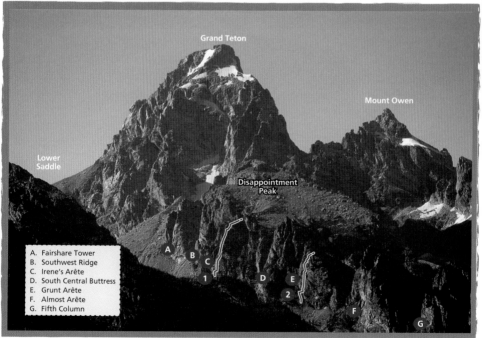

A. Fairshare Tower
B. Southwest Ridge
C. Irene's Arête
D. South Central Buttress
E. Grunt Arête
F. Almost Arête
G. Fifth Column

Climbing the third pitch of the
classic route *Irene's Arête.*

activity, but the main attraction is the long row of south-facing arêtes and buttresses directly above the Garnet Canyon Trail. Many routes have been done on these features due to this proximity and their warm southern exposure. While some of these routes have fallen into obscurity, a few have withstood the test of time and now are considered classics. Of them all, a solitary line stands out and has gained a wide reputation as one of the best rock climbs in the Tetons. Long before most climbers make their first journey to these mountains, they are aware of a route called *Irene's Arête*.

1. Irene's Arête (III 5.8 or 5.10a) An unusually sharp, clean fin of rock draws the eye from the other features on the northern skyline as one hikes westward from the Platforms in Garnet Canyon. This is Irene's Arête, which was first climbed by John Dietschy and Irene Ortenburger on July 10, 1957. The route is not terribly difficult, but the climbing is fairly sustained, the rock is beautiful and, unlike many other Teton outings, there are no scrambling pitches. The more difficult "direct" variations are credited to Jim Olson and Mark Chapman from an ascent on July 2, 1970.

Approach: Hike the Garnet Canyon Trail to the point where it officially ends at Garnet Creek in the narrows of the canyon. The Platforms campsite is just across the stream to the south. The Climbers' Trail continues up Garnet Canyon to the west in a jumble of giant boulders. Hike the Climbers' Trail all the way to the last of some eighteen switchbacks above the Meadows. Continue west past a cliff on the right, and about 150 feet farther before reaching the top of Spalding Falls, turn right on a footpath that climbs steeply up talus to the north. Work back around to the top of the cliff where a broad, wooded ledge leads about 200 yards east to the base of Irene's Arête. The initial grove of trees is a good place to leave extra gear. Follow the ledge down around the foot of a small buttress and up the far side to a notch with a large pine tree. This point is below and just east of Irene's Arête. Turn north, then work up and left along ramps and short cliffs to a ledge that is just west of the continuous aspect of the arête (Class 4). This point can also be reached from the higher forested ledge beneath the Caves Arête.

The Route
Belay on the ledge or pull around onto the east side of the arête and belay atop a pedestal.

Pitch 1: Climb discontinuous cracks (5.7) and belay in an alcove beside a strange block with a "finger" that points up and left (100 feet). **Pitch 2:** Jam a steep hand crack with fixed pins (5.8) and belay on a big ledge (100 feet). Move the belay north to the base of the arête. **Pitch 3:** Climb about

Caves Arête and Irene's Arête from Garnet Canyon

10 feet just left of the crest, then pull around to the right into a marginal crack system (5.7). Work straight up a dihedral in black rock, pull around to the left side of the crest, and jam another 30 feet up to a good ledge on the right side of the crest (5.7, 165 feet). Pitch 3 **Variation:** Begin down to the right from the arête in an area of white, decomposed rock. Jam a crack up through a roof (5.9) and merge left with the regular line. **Pitch 4:** Make strenuous moves up and left past a fixed pin (5.8), then climb beautiful, steep rock along the arête to a black roof (5.6). Pull right into the middle of the roof, crank up on big jugs, and exit the roof at a 2-inch white crystal (5.8). Continue up into a groove (5.7) and work slightly left to belay on a good ledge at the base of a 90-degree dihedral (160 feet). Pitch 4 **variation 1:** Begin just right of the belay and jam a finger crack up to the black roof (5.8). Pitch 4 **variation 2:** At the roof it is possible to stay left and climb the arête (5.7, no pro) to the belay. **Pitch 5:** Jam and stem up the dihedral (5.9), hand traverse up and right, then power up a groove (5.7) to a lower-angle section of the arête. Run the rope all the way to the notch at the next vertical step and belay (165 feet). Pitch 5 **variation 1:** Work around to the left of the dihedral and up to the arête (5.7). Pitch 5 **variation 2:** Pull right around the arête and climb a good crack up to the low-angle section (5.8). **Pitch 6:** Although

there are easier alternatives, the direct finish is well protected and is the line of choice. From the highest point, stem across the gap to the vertical wall and undercling/lieback up into a dihedral that is followed to the end of the roped climbing (5.10a, 70 feet). A #3.5 Friend or equivalent is useful here. Pitch 6 **variation 1:** Move down the gully about 60 feet to the east and climb a steep fist crack to scrambling terrain (5.8). Pitch 6 **variation 2:** Descend the gully about 150 feet to the east and make a few steep moves (5.5) to reach a low-angle slab, then scramble northwest to the ridge crest.

Rack: Full gear up to 3 inches.

Descent A: Scramble along the crest of the ridge, first on the right then on the left to avoid a tower. Once on the slopes of Disappointment Peak, follow a faint path westward through scrub evergreens to the second gully west of Irene's Arête. This is the *Southwest Couloir* (Class 4), and it is the easiest way to return to the Caves area and the base of the climb. About a third of the way down the gully, the descent is blocked by a large chockstone. Rappel 60 feet from slings or pass it by scrambling across to the east and downclimbing an easy chimney. Continue down the steep, loose gully staying mostly to the right, but avoid a right branch that leads more to the west.

Descent B: Hike down to the east, to a plateau that is above and southwest of Amphitheater Lake. Stay to the south of the Spoon Couloir (the long, narrow gully) and descend to the east via ledges and short cliffs until it is possible to curve around north to the lake. Find the Amphitheater Lake Trail (aka Glacier Trail) at the east end of the lake and follow it to its junction with the Garnet Canyon Trail (see the *Lake Ledges* route below). The Grand Teton quad will be useful when making this descent for the first time.

2. Open Book (III 5.9) The South Central Buttress forms a large summit that rises above the skyline of the ridge a thousand feet or more to the right (east) of Irene's Arête. The next feature to the right of this is called Grunt Arête, perhaps for the route of the same name, or perhaps the other way around. About 100 feet right of this arête, a large open-book dihedral splits the face and poses a fine rock climb. The long crack system in the corner of the dihedral was first climbed by Philip Jacobus and Steve Larsen on August 21, 1963. The first all free ascent was made by Jim Donini and

Disappointment Peak—*Irene's Arete*

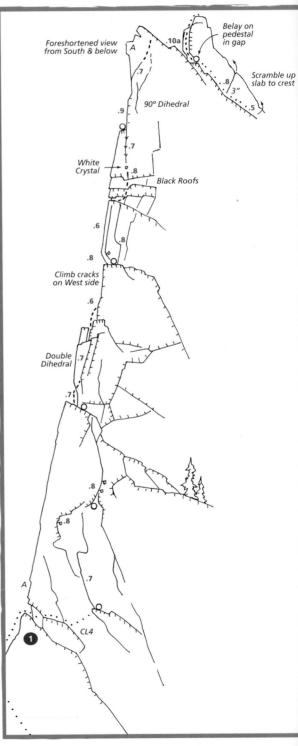

Foreshortened view
from South & below

Belay on
pedestal
in gap

Scramble up
slab to crest

.10a

.7

A

.8

3″

.5

90° Dihedral

.9

.7

White
Crystal

.8

Black Roofs

.6

.8

.8

Climb cracks
on West side

.6

Double
Dihedral

.7

.7

.8

.8

.7

A

CL4

…on Cassidy on *Open Book* (III 5.9),
…pointment Peak.
GREG VON DOERSTEN

Disappointment Peak, Grunt Arête—*Open Book*

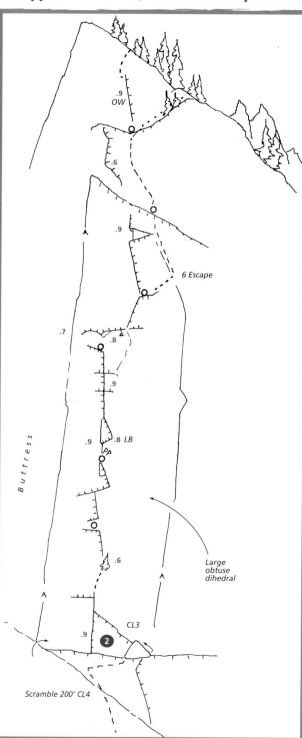

Mike Munger on June 26, 1977.

Approach: Hike the Garnet Canyon Trail to the point where it officially ends at Garnet Creek in the narrows of the canyon. The Platforms campsite is just across the stream to the south. The Climbers' Trail continues up Garnet Canyon to the west in a jumble of giant boulders. Grunt Arête and the *Open Book* are plainly visible up to the north from this point. Hike talus and easy ledges to the west of the arête, then traverse right onto a big ledge at the bottom of the dihedral. It is also possible to hike up a ramp from the east.

The Route

Belay at a big flake to the right of the corner.

Pitch 1: Climb up and left along a ramp (Class 3) or take a more difficult direct start to the left (5.9). Climb straight up past a small tree and belay beneath a roof (5.6).

Pitch 2: Climb up and pass a roof on the right (5.8) via undercling and lieback, then belay above a detached flake from two pins. **Pitch 3:** Climb around either side of a flake (easier on the right), then continue up a thin crack past two small roofs (5.9) and belay on a ledge beneath a large overhang. **Pitch 4:** Traverse about 20 feet right beneath the roof until it is possible to escape upward at an exposed slot (5.8). It may be possible to pass this roof on the left (5.7). Climb a short left-facing dihedral and belay. It is possible to escape the route by climbing up and right from this belay (5.5 or 5.6). **Pitch 5:** Continue up the left-facing dihedral and turn a roof on the left (5.9). Belay above on a good ledge. **Pitch 6:** Continue up the same corner system (5.6) to another ledge where you can scramble off to the right. **Pitch 7:** Climb a rotten left-facing dihedral with a wide crack to the top of the face (5.9).

Rack: Full rock gear up to 3 inches.

Descent: Traverse north from the top of the climb, then drop down to the east. Downclimb a chimney past some chockstones and descend a large gully south into Garnet Canyon. It is perhaps easier to scramble down to Surprise Lake and follow its outlet south into Garnet Canyon or hike out via the Amphitheater Trail (aka Glacier Trail).

3. Lake Ledges (II Class 4) No topo. This is the route taken on the first ascent of Disappointment Peak as mentioned above. Hike straight west from Amphitheater Lake and scramble up through cliffs and ledges following the line of least resistance for about 500 feet. The usual line of ascent lies a short way left of the Spoon Couloir, the narrow gully that splits the cliff. When filled with snow, this gully is a good moderate snow climb. Hike northwest from the top of the cliffs, up the long talus slope, and scramble up easy rock to the summit.

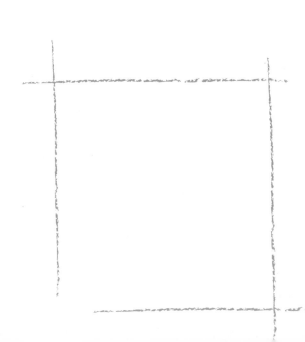

Mount Owen

Mount Owen (12,928 feet) is the second highest of the Teton summits. It is completely eclipsed by Teewinot Mountain from the southeast shore of Jenny Lake, but is quite striking from other vantages. Its most famous profile is perhaps from the northeast where it nearly obscures the Grand Teton in a dramatic cluster of peaks known as the Cathedral Group. Mount Owen forms the north wall of the Teton Glacier cirque. It is connected to the Grand Teton via Gunsight Notch and the Grandstand and is connected to Teewinot by a long ridge to the east. This graceful diadem of jagged ridges and terraced snowfields was the last of the great Teton peaks to be climbed, and its first ascent by the *East Ridge* created one of the finest alpine routes in the range.

1. East Ridge (II 5.6) This aesthetic and satisfying route ascends a deep couloir to a col on the east ridge, then continues up terraced snowfields and the prominent upper buttress to the summit. The ascent develops tremendous relief and scenic grandeur as one moves up the final pitches toward the summit knob. The north

Grand Teton and Mount Owen from the East

Climbers on the *East Ridge* of Mount Owen (II 5.6) at sunrise.
PHOTO GREG VON DOERSTEN

Mount Owen from the Southeast

face of the Grand Teton looms larger than life to the south across the void of the Teton Glacier, while the southwest ridge of Storm Point appears in miniature 5,500 feet below to the north. The route was first climbed by Kenneth Henderson, Robert Underhill, Phil Smith, and Fritiof Fryxell on July 16, 1930.

Approach: At a signed junction 3 miles up the Garnet Canyon Trail, the Amphitheater Lake Trail (aka Glacier Trail) continues straight ahead where the Garnet Canyon Trail cuts back to the left. Hike the Glacier Trail to Surprise Lake, which is the traditional campsite for the ascent. It is also possible to camp in the moraine beneath the east ridge of the Grand Teton. Continue to Amphitheater Lake and pick up a climber's path that leads north to a notch in the east ridge of Disappointment Peak where Mount Owen comes into full view. Descend 150 feet to the north, then traverse west along a ledge into Glacier Gulch. Contour around to the north and climb the moraine onto the Teton Glacier.

The Route

Cross the lower Teton Glacier and enter the initial section of the *Koven Couloir,* the obvious gully that leads to the col west of the East Prong. Kick steps in snow (scree in late season) up to a small waterfall. Pass this feature on the left and attain a broad, typically snow-covered bench. Above

the bench, climb the steeper upper couloir to the col west of the East Prong, either directly up steep snow or via fourth-class terrain on the left side of the couloir. Head straight west and encounter the next obstacle, a 120-foot rock band. Traverse about 50 feet north from the crest of the ridge and climb a deep chimney to the upper snowfield. The chockstone near the top of the chimney may be passed on either side.

The climb becomes more dramatic from here. Ascend the eastern crest of the snowfield to the base of the upper east ridge where several options exist for passing the steep initial buttress. **Option 1:** Perhaps the easiest is to continue on snow for several hundred feet along the north side of the ridge until it is possible to work up and left along ramps and ledges to the ridge crest. **Option 2:** A more difficult and aesthetic option is to climb directly up the east arête of the buttress via a 60-foot left-facing dihedral (5.7) that leads to a belay at a fixed pin. Traverse about 20 feet right from the belay and scramble a full rope-length up a shallow gully (Class 4) that leads to the ridge crest. **Option 3:** Climb an obvious and moderate chimney system on the south side of the ridge (see topo).

Proceed west along the crest of the ridge for a couple of hundred feet to a ledge with slings. Climb a moderate gully on the south side of the crest for a full rope length to

Mount Owen from the Southeast

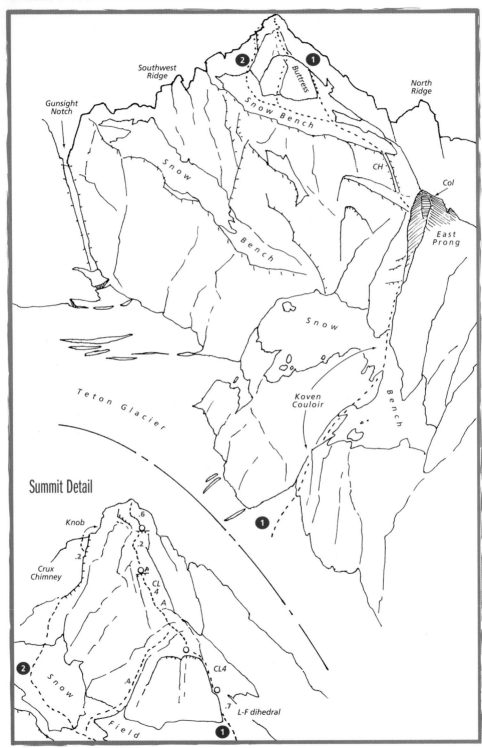

Southwest Ridge

North Ridge

Gunsight Notch

Buttress

Snow Bench

CH

Col

S n o w

East Prong

B e n c h

S n o w

T e t o n   G l a c i e r

Koven Couloir

B e n c h

Summit Detail

Knob

.6

.2

Crux Chimney

.2

CL 4 A

CL4

.4

.7

L-F dihedral

S n o w   F i e l d

an alcove at the base of the summit knob. The final event is a steep, 60-foot slab. Begin this last pitch to the right, work up and left to a small flake (5.6), traverse left on a downsloping ledge, then shoot straight for the top. The last 30 feet are easier.

Rack: Ice axe, mountain boots, crampons, and a modest rock rack up to 2 inches.

Descent: It is relatively easy to rappel the *East Ridge* and the *Koven Couloir,* as a series of sling anchors exist for this purpose. Two ropes are required. It also is not difficult to downclimb the *Koven Route* beginning on the west side of the summit knob.

2. Koven Route (II 5.2) Theodore and Gustav Koven, Paul Petzoldt, and Glen Exum reached the summit on July 20, 1931, by a variation of the original *East Ridge,* and thus discovered the easiest route up Mount Owen. This is a sweeping snow climb in early to midsummer with a short stretch of rock at the top; more rock and scree will have to be negotiated in late season.

The Route

Begin with the *East Ridge* and follow it all the way to the upper snowfield. Traverse left along the bench below the upper buttress of the *East Ridge,* all the way to slabs and ledges near the southwest ridge. Head northwest up a gully to a steep corner. Ascend a 40-foot chimney in the right wall (crux), then move left up steep slabs to reach the crest of the southwest ridge. Follow an easy ledge system north to an area of black rock. Work up and right to the base of a deep chimney that leads to the summit in 40 feet.

3. Serendipity Arête (IV 5.7) This provocative route ascends the steep western arête of Mount Owen, which viewed from the *Black Ice Couloir* forms the left skyline of the peak. The pinnacled arête can be identified by a large, crescent-shaped left-facing dihedral on its lower buttress and by its termination at the highest tower along the north ridge. William Buckingham, Rick Medrick, Sterling Neale, and Frank Magary completed the first ascent on August 8, 1959. Henry Mitchell and George Griffin made the first free ascent on July 14, 1965.

Approach: Hike about 3 miles up the Cascade Canyon Trail (see under Cascade Canyon Crags, page 97) to a point just west of the drainage from Valhalla Canyon. The northwest side of the Grand Teton is visible from here. Ford Cascade Creek (a log crossing may be available a bit upstream from the confluence) and follow a rugged climber's path up the steep, forested slope, staying to the right of the stream, into Valhalla Canyon. Hike into the upper reaches of Valhalla Canyon until directly beneath Gunsight Notch, the sharp break in

Mount Owen from the Southwest

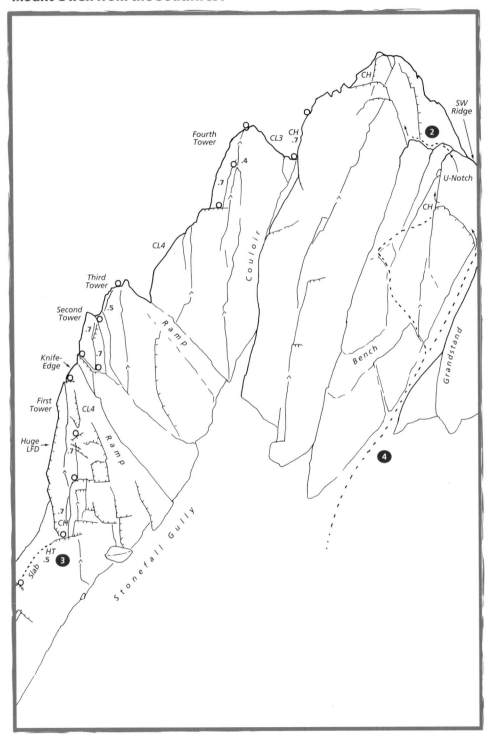

the ridge between Mount Owen and the Grand Teton. Turn east and climb snow or scree up the *West Gunsight Couloir* until it is possible to traverse left (north) above a smaller gully onto a large scree bench above a cliffband. It also is possible to scramble up the smaller gully. Look for a bivouac platform beneath the rib separating the small gully from the *West Gunsight Couloir*. Continue north along the bench to the bottom of the main buttress, just past a stonefall gully that descends from a distinct U-shaped notch in the ridge crest.

The Route

Scramble up slabs for several hundred feet to the base of the first steep tower. Traverse up and left across broken ledges for half a rope length to start the first hard pitch. Intermediate belays can be made on some of the longer pitches.

Pitch 1: Climb straight up past the left end of a small roof (5.4), hand traverse right along the top of a slab, and continue right around the crest to the base of a shallow chimney (5.5). **Pitch 2:** Climb the chimney for about 30 feet, step left, and jam a clean crack until it is possible to move back into the chimney (5.7) and continue to a good ledge. **Pitch 3:** Climb straight up a slab, jam a hand crack through a roof (5.7), and belay above on a ledge. Scramble to the top of the first tower (Class 4). **Pitch 4:** Traverse a spectacular knife-edge ridge to the base of the smaller

second tower and belay on a ledge (5.4). **Pitch 5:** Traverse 35 feet down and right along a narrow ledge and belay beneath a crack and chimney system in black rock. **Pitch 6:** Jam and stem up the cracks and belay in the notch behind the second tower (5.7). **Pitch 7:** Climb an easy crack above the belay to gain the top of the third tower (5.5). Scramble several hundred feet up the left side of the crest and gain a big ledge at the base of the fourth tower. **Pitch 8:** Climb a fist crack on the north side of the arête and belay at a stance after 150 feet (5.7). **Pitch 9:** Scramble up easy rock on the right side of the crest to the top of the fourth tower (5.4). This is the highest tower on the north ridge of Mount Owen. Scramble down to the col between the fourth tower and the summit block. **Pitch 10:** Climb a steep chimney that may require an aid move (5.7, A0 or 5.9). Follow the north ridge for several hundred feet to the summit or traverse out onto the west face and climb the west chimney of the *Koven Route* (Class 4).

Rack: Full gear up to 3.5 inches.

Descent: There are at least three ways to descend from the summit: (1) Downclimb and rappel the *East Ridge;* (2) downclimb the *Koven Route* (see above) and escape to the east in either case; or (3) downclimb the *West Ledges* (II 5.2) route, best if a camp was left in Valhalla Canyon: Downclimb the *Koven Route* to the point along the southwest ridge where it descends to the east. Work south

Mount Owen and Grand Teton from the West

along the east side of the southwest ridge to a distinct U-notch between two towers. Do not start down the west side of the southwest ridge too soon; rappel slings facilitating this blunder are found along the crest. Ignore these and continue to the distinct U-notch between two towers. Descend a chimney, traverse south, then downclimb the west slabs as shown in the photo. With good navigating the entire descent can be made without rappels.

4. West Ledges (II 5.2) This moderate route is more useful as a descent than a climbing objective due to its long, arduous approach via Valhalla Canyon. It was first climbed by Paul Petzoldt and Edward Woolf on July 28, 1932. Approach as for *Serendipity Arête* and gain the far south end of the scree bench. Climb to the base of a steep wall of dark rock, then work up and left to a long couloir that descends from a distinct U-notch in the crest of the southwest ridge. Do not climb the couloir; instead, work up and right over slabs to a point just short of the ridge crest. Traverse left and climb a chimney to the U-notch. Continue along the east side of the crest and finish as for *Koven Route*.

Teewinot Mountain

Teewinot (12,325 feet) is one of the most beautiful and compelling peaks in the Tetons. It is the only alpine peak wholly visible from the main visitor area at Jenny Lake. Its prominent position along the eastern slope of the range, directly above the Lupine Meadows parking area, makes Teewinot the most accessible of the major Teton summits.

1. East Face (II 5.2 AI2) A rough trail wanders up a triangular, timbered ridge called the Apex that stretches far up into the middle of Teewinot's east face. A broad couloir slashes up and right above tree line to a notch at the south side of the summit. These features define the *East Face,* which is among the most direct and enjoyable alpine outings in the Tetons.

Teewinot Mountain as seen from the east shore of Jenny Lake.

Teewinot Mountain, East Face

What it lacks in technical challenge is more than offset by the brevity of approach, direct line to the summit, and peerless views of the Grand Teton and Mount Owen. The route is a long snow climb in early season, but the 5,600-foot ascent may go entirely on rock by mid-August. Fritiof Fryxell and Phil Smith made the first documented ascent on August 14, 1929.

The Route

The Apex Trail begins along the west side of the Lupine Meadows parking area about 150 feet from its north end. Follow this trail westward through a tangle of scrub vegetation then up the forested ridge. The trail reaches tree line and the top of the Apex after an interminable number of switchbacks. The path veers right and

Samantha Worthington on the summit of Teewinot Mountain.
PHOTO GREG VON DOERSTEN

Teewinot Mountain, East Face

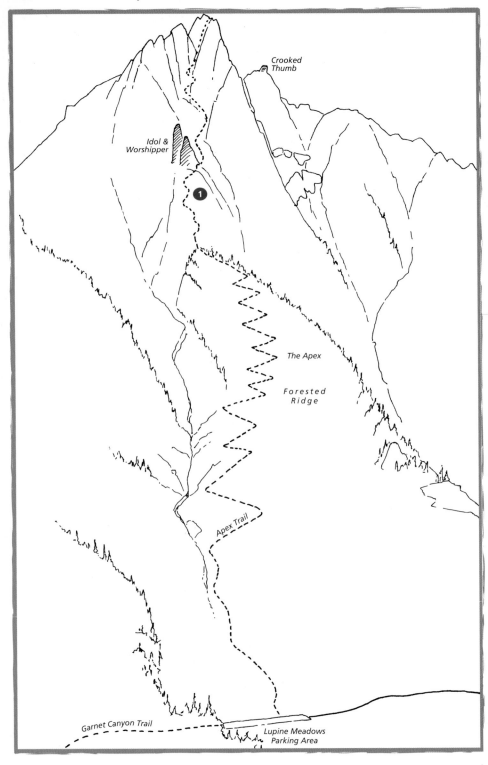

Crooked Thumb

Idol & Worshipper

1

The Apex

Forested Ridge

Apex Trail

Garnet Canyon Trail

Lupine Meadows Parking Area

climbs steeply to a talus field beneath two prominent gendarmes known as the Worshipper and the Idol. Angle up and right into the broad couloir where snow travel is likely to begin. In late season, look for a vague path up ramps and gullies with sections of easy rock climbing. The final stretch of the couloir narrows and holds a finger of perennial snow. Break right about 300 feet below the top of the couloir.

Work up and right on moderate rock (or snow) to the ridge crest where a short scramble west leads to the tiny exposed summit and into the very heart of the Tetons.

Rack: Ice axe, mountain boots, crampons, rope, and a light rock rack. Some parties may want to belay the steeper sections above the snow couloir.

Descent: Reverse the route.

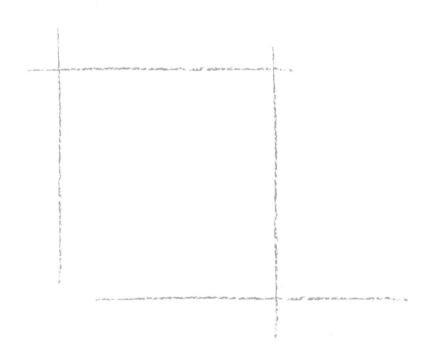

Joyce Rossiter on the sixth pitch of *Guide's Wall*, Southwest Ridge of Storm Point.

3.

Cascade Canyon Crags

Teton approaches are sometimes more arduous than the routes to which they lead, so any good crag or peak with a short approach is bound to be popular. The main routes on Storm Point, Symmetry Spire, Cube Point, and Baxter Pinnacle have for many years been the standard "crag climbs" in the range. These climbs are graced with short approaches, beautiful rock, commanding vistas, and relatively uncomplicated descents.

Getting there: The approaches can be made still shorter by taking the shuttle boat across Jenny Lake. Information on departures and boarding fees is available at the Jenny Lake Ranger Station or at the boat dock, a short walk southwest from the ranger station. Printable maps that illustrate the vast network of trails in Grand Teton National Park are available at www.nps.gov/grte/planyourvisit/hike.htm.

Cascade Canyon looking West across Jenny Lake

Cascade Canyon Crags and Trails from the Southeast

TRAILS AND APPROACHES

Valley Trail

This important trail runs on a north-south axis all the way from Teton Village to Trapper Lake. Some length of the Valley Trail must be hiked or crossed to reach the climbs described in this chapter. The trail is reached from the Jenny Lake or String Lake Trailheads or by taking the shuttle boat across Jenny Lake. It runs along the west shore of Jenny Lake and the east shores of String Lake and Leigh Lake.

Cascade Canyon Trail

This popular trail begins from the Valley Trail a short way north or south of the shuttle boat dock on the west shore of Jenny Lake and provides access to Teewinot Mountain (north side), Mount Owen (north side), Valhalla Canyon, Storm Point, Symmetry Couloir, Symmetry Spire, and Baxter Pinnacle. There are three ways to reach the Cascade Canyon Trail:

1. Take the shuttle boat across Jenny Lake. Follow a signed trail to Hidden Falls and reach Inspiration Point (7,200 feet) barely a mile from the dock.
2. Begin from the Jenny Lake Trailhead (near the marina) and hike around the south and west sides of the lake. A left branch leads to Hidden Falls and reaches Inspiration Point 2.4 miles from the trailhead.
3. Begin from the String Lake Trailhead and hike the Valley Trail along the northwest side of Jenny Lake to the Horse Trail (1.7 miles). Follow the Horse Trail west below Baxter Pinnacle and reach the Cascade Canyon Trail 0.7 mile from the Valley Trail.

The Cascade Canyon Trail goes west from Inspiration Point and reaches the Cascade Canyon Forks 4.1 miles from the Valley Trail . The right branch follows the North Fork of Cascade Canyon and reaches Lake Solitude (9,035 feet), 6.8 miles from the Valley Trail. The left branch follows the South Fork of Cascade Canyon and reaches Hurricane Pass just north of the Schoolroom Glacier (about 10,380 feet), 9.2 miles from the Valley Trail. A left branch in the valley bottom, beneath the Schoolroom Glacier, follows an undeveloped trail south to the unnamed pass between The Wall and the west ridge of the South Teton (10,560+ feet).

Horse Trail

The Horse Trail begins from the Valley Trail about 300 yards north of the shuttle boat dock on the west side of Jenny Lake and maybe 200 yards south of the drainage from Hanging Canyon. The trail climbs west through the trees, then contours around to the south and joins the Cascade Canyon Trail where it levels off west of

Inspiration Point, 0.7 mile from the Valley Trail. The Horse Trail is a good shortcut to the Cascade Canyon Trail if you are hiking south from String Lake and provides access to Baxter Pinnacle and Symmetry Couloir along the way.

Hanging Canyon Trail

This important footpath has in recent years been improved by the National Park Service. The narrow but distinct trail begins from the Valley Trail in the trees, a short way northeast of the main drainage from Hanging Canyon (about 250 yards north of the Horse Trail). The beginning of the trail is unsigned and is easy to miss. Look for a row of stones on the west side of the Valley Trail about 100 feet north of a wooden foot bridge. The path heads northwest through brush and windfall to the open meadow beneath Ribbon Cascade. It makes a big switchback on the north slope, curves around to the south above Ribbon Cascade and climbs west beneath Cube Point into the upper canyon. The path ends at Ramshead Lake (c. 9460) beneath the north face of Symmetry Spire.

Laurel Lake Way Trail

It is possible to reach Hanging Canyon from the southwest side of String Lake. Begin from the String Lake Trailhead and hike the Valley Trail south to the first junction (0.3 mile). Go right on the Paintbrush Canyon Trail, cross the outlet stream from Laurel Lake, and continue north a short way. Leave the trail and follow a vague path southwest up an open slope to Laurel Lake. Hike a bit higher, then contour south and reach Hanging Canyon at the level of Arrowhead Pool. (A "way trail" is a path developed by foot traffic, not built by a trail crew.)

Symmetry Couloir

The big gully between Storm Point and Symmetry Spire is the usual approach to the summits of Storm Point, Ice Point, Symmetry Spire and to rock climbs on the south face of the latter. A rugged path weaves up the couloir, almost a climb in its own right, and leads to Symmetry Col, the saddle between Ice Point and Symmetry Spire (about 9,700 feet). An ice axe, mountain boots and crampons are needed until mid to late summer when most of the couloir is finally free of snow. Do not underestimate the hazzard of snow travel in this couloir, which has been the scene of many accidents.

Hike the Valley Trail to the Horse Trail (about 0.25 mile north of the boat dock). Follow the Horse Trail west through forest and beneath Baxter's Pinnacle to where it levels off and crosses an alluvial fan with a stream. Just before crossing the stream, a climber's path goes right (west) and leads up brushy talus to a cliffband that blocks access to the upper couloir. Follow the path into an aclove in

Symmetry Couloir, Showing More than 1500 Feet of Hard Surfaced Snow, July 28, 2011

the cliff with a small waterfall. Climb the cliff on the left (Class 4) above a big boulder, right of the waterfall, and gain a ledge system that runs west above the cliff. Follow a rough path along the cliff and cross to the left side of the drainage where the cliff fades. Continue up the left side of the couloir for a 1000 feet to an upper cliff that is passed on the left. Move right where the terrain opens and hike up a steep path that leads to the saddle between Ice Point and Symmetry Spire. Break right below the saddle to reach climbs on the south face of Symmetry Spire.

STORM POINT

Storm Point (10,054 feet) is the massive crag south of Symmetry Spire and across Cascade Canyon from Teewinot Mountain. Its pointed summit is readily visible from the east shore of Jenny Lake with Ice Point and the much larger Symmetry Spire to the right. Many routes have been completed over the years on Storm Point, though among them only *Guide's Wall* has become popular or is even known to most climbers.

1. Guide's Wall (III 5.8 to 5.10c)
Guide's Wall is the name given to the first nine pitches of the *Southwest Ridge* route on Storm Point. The original line follows the entire 3,000-foot ridge to the summit and requires about forty pitches. Now only the first six pitches are normally climbed. The

Southwest Ridge was first climbed by Richard Pownall and Art Gilkey during the summer of 1949; more difficult variations have been developed since then by different parties.

Approach: Hike the Cascade Canyon Trail to where a rock slide has caused the formation of a large pond (about 1.5 miles west of Inspiration Point). The southwest ridge of Storm Point is directly north from the east end of the pond. Hike up the rock slide to the first cliffband, scramble right across a convenient ledge, follow a steep path up and right, then go west to the top of a ramp.

The Route

From the top of the ramp, scramble left behind a tree, go up a steeper ramp to a ledge on the west side of the arête, and set the belay. **Pitch 1:** Climb a right-facing dihedral with a fixed pin (5.7) and follow cracks and corners to a two-bolt anchor 15 feet above an obvious ledge (120 feet). Pitch 1 **Variation:** Start behind the initial tree. Climb a roof (5.10a) and the clean dihedrals above to the two-bolt anchor. **Pitch 2:** Climb an undistinguished pitch with harder variations to the right or left (5.7) and belay on a broad ledge with some trees (100 feet). **Pitch 3:** Climb a long left-facing dihedral on the left side of the arête and belay at its top (5.7, 100 feet). Pitch 3 **Variation:** Move right from the trees and belay at two boulders. Climb a steep finger crack with

pitons (5.8) to a ledge, pull over a roof (5.7), and continue up easier terrain to a ledge with a small tree (100 feet). **Pitch 4:** Climb a short, easy pitch to Flake Ledge, a long terrace that wraps around the arête and is characterized by a 30-foot spike of rock. **Pitch 5:** Climb twin cracks just right of the spike (5.7) and belay at a stance just past the left end of a big roof (80 feet). Pitch 5 **Variation 1:** Climb the exquisite finger/hand crack a few feet to the right of the double cracks and merge left at the roof (5.9+). It is also possible to turn the roof at a spike (5.10b/c). Pitch 5 **Variation 2:** Begin

to the left of the spike and tackle a right-facing flake/crack (5.10c). **Pitch 6:** Continue up a shallow dihedral and a thin crack with fixed pins (5.8+), then step left on a ledge and belay from a two-bolt anchor.

Rack: Standard rack up to 2 inches.

Descent: Make the first of four long rappels from the bolt anchor at the top of the sixth pitch. Note that the second and third rappels are from trees and that a short traverse southward along a ledge is required to reach the final bolt anchor 150 feet above the start of the climb.

Ice Point and Storm Point Viewed from Col 10300 at the Top of the Southwest Couloir on Symmetry Spire

2. Upper West Face (II Class 4) This is the easiest way to reach the summit of Storm Point and is often combined with an ascent on Ice Point. It was first climbed by Fritiof Fryxell and Frank Smith on August 13, 1931. Approach via the *Symmetry Couloir* and gain the saddle between Symmetry Spire and Ice Point. Climb Ice Point as described below or follow ledges around its west side to the col between Ice Point and Storm Point. Climb directly up the north ridge of Storm Point for 50 feet, then follow a broad ledge that traverses out onto the west face. Climb a short corner at the end of the ledge, then continue up easier terrain to the summit.

ICE POINT

Ice Point (9,920+ feet) is the elegant little spire along the ridge between Storm Point and Symmetry Spire. Its north shoulder forms the south side of the Ice Point–Symmetry Spire saddle.

1. Northwest Ridge (I Class 4) An ascent of the *Northwest Ridge* is often combined with an ascent of the *Upper West Face* of Storm Point. The first ascent was made by Fritiof Fryxell and Frank Smith on August 13, 1931. Approach via the *Symmetry Couloir* and gain the saddle between Ice Point and Symmetry Spire. Follow the ridge crest south, staying a bit on the

Ice Point from the South

east side. Gain a notch in the steeper west ridge and follow the narrow crest to the summit. From the notch in the ridge, it is easy to descend the *Southwest Ridge* route to the saddle between Ice Point and Storm Point (Class 4) and climb the *Upper West Face* to the summit of Storm Point.

2. Southwest Ridge (I Class 4) This is the easiest way to climb or descend Ice Point. Begin from the talus on the southwest side of the spire. Climb a ramp that angles up and left to the notch on ridge crest. Continue as for the *Northwest Ridge*.

3. South Ridge (I 5.5) This route ascends the far right side of the southwest face, which could be described as the south ridge. History of the route is unknown. Data is from an ascent by the author on July 28, 2011. Begin from the highest point of talus beneath the southwest face. Step off from a boulder and climb straight up the west side of the ridge. Pull through some blocks at the top of a short dihedral and move right. Step across to a crack on the east side of the ridge and climb straight up to a big ledge. Climb a short, steep wall and pull up over the crest of the ridge. Walk to the summit.

 Descent: Downclimb the *Southwest Ridge*.

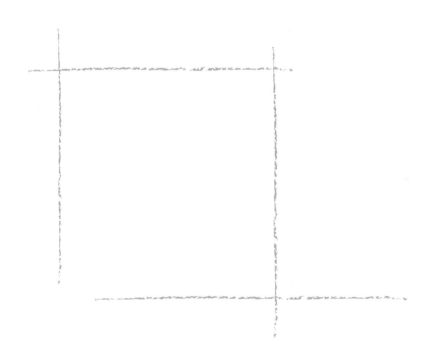

Symmetry Spire from the Southeast

Symmetry Spire

2

3

4

Cube Point

2

Hanging Canyon

Symmetry Couloir

Baxter Pinnacle

Cascade Canyon

1

SYMMETRY SPIRE

Symmetry Spire (10,560+ feet) is the most prominent feature in the group of summits at the east end of the ridge between Cascade Canyon and Hanging Canyon. It is easily recognized from Jenny Lake by its double south buttress. The approaches are somewhat arduous, but the climbing is superb and the *Southwest Ridge* is one of the best moderate rock climbs in the Tetons.

South Face of Symmetry Spire from the Summit of Ice Point

Col 10300

Symmetry Couloir

Approach A: Climb the *Symmetry Couloir* to the saddle between Ice Point and Symmetry Spire, then traverse right to routes on the south face. An ice axe, mountain boots and crampons are needed until mid to late summer.

Approach B: Hike the Hanging Canyon Trail to Ramshead Lake and the north face of Symmetry Spire which is also the approach to Cube Point.

Descent from all routes: From the summit, downclimb the *Northwest Ledges* (Class 4) to Col 10300 (on the west side of the peak), then continue down the *Southwest Couloir* or the *Northwest Couloir*. It also is possible to rappel 75 feet west into the *Southwest Couloir* from a gap in the ridge below the last steep section along the crest of the *Southwest Ridge;* look for a sling anchor. Both descents require an ice axe, mountain boots and crampons until late summer when the seasonal snow is gone.

1. Southwest Couloir (II Class 4) This route provides an easy method of reaching the summit as well as the usual line of descent on the south side. It was first climbed by Eldon Petzoldt on July 8, 1935. From Symmetry Col, at the top of the *Symmetry Couloir,* hike north on snow or scree and ascend the steep couloir along the western margin of Symmetry Spire for about 600 feet to Col 10300. Scramble east up the ridge for about 100 feet then follow ledges out onto the upper

north face. From here a path zigzags up ledges to the summit. The section above the col is the old *Northwest Ledges* route.

Rack: Ice axe, mountain boots and crampons are needed until most of the seasonal snow is gone.

Descent: Reverse the route.

2. Southwest Ridge (II 5.7) The southwest ridge rises steeply to the right of the *Southwest Couloir* and poses one of the best moderate rock climbs in the Tetons. This great route was established by Bert Jensen and Walter Spofford on July 30, 1938.

The Route

Begin at the bottom of the ridge among some small trees or about 100 feet up to the left. **Pitches 1 and 2:** Climb steep but moderate rock for two pitches and gain a broken ledge system in dark rock beneath a steep wall with several right-facing dihedrals (5.4). Belay on the highest ledge at right. **Pitch 3:** Climb the third dihedral from the left straight up to a ledge (5.6, 120 feet). Pitch 3 **Variation:** Start up the third dihedral, but traverse right into the next corner and climb to the same ledge (5.5). **Pitch 4:** Climb straight up a "nose" of golden rock past some fixed pins and belay on a ledge (5.7) or run the rope out to the next belay. The nose can be avoided by traversing around it on the right. **Pitch 5:** From the belay above the nose, climb straight up

Symmetry Spire from Base of *Southwest Ridge*

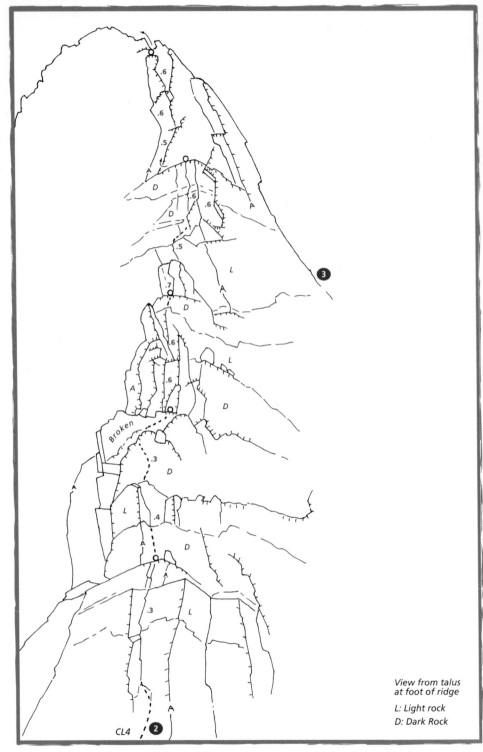

View from talus
at foot of ridge

L: Light rock
D: Dark Rock

dark rock to the left of the crest and belay on a big ledge (5.5). Pitch 5 **Variation:** From the top of the nose, work up and right to the crest and follow a shallow corner on the right to the big ledge. **Pitch 6:** Step down to the left and climb a steep ramp that angles up and right (5.5). Belay at its top or continue up through the next pitch. **Pitch 7:** Climb a steep face of dark rock and negotiate a steep flake either by climbing the chimney along its right side or the face on the left (5.6). Belay atop the flake. Cross to the right side of the ridge and follow the crest to the summit.

3. Durrance Ridge (II 5.6) Several hundred feet to the east of *Southwest Ridge,* a deep couloir known as *Templeton's Crack* splits the south face of Symmetry Spire; the route on the long ridge that forms the left side of this couloir is called *Durrance Ridge.* This is an easier climb than the *Southwest Ridge* that features excellent, steep rock with solid protection,

good belays—and ten pitches of climbing. Jack Durrance and Walter Spofford made the first ascent on August 7, 1936.

The Route
Begin at the very foot of the ridge, adjacent to Templeton's Crack. Climb several moderate pitches on the crest of the ridge to a steep 25-foot wall about halfway up. Climb a crack with a fixed pin (5.5) to pass the wall, then continue on easier ground for about 200 feet (Class 4) to where the angle steepens. A final challenge remains to be surmounted: Just left of the ridge crest, climb a long crack system with some fixed pins (5.6) and a short chimney that leads to the ridge top. Beware of a loose chockstone on this pitch. Climb up and left (west) to the upper *Southwest Ridge* and follow the crest to the summit.

Rack: Standard rack up to 2.5 inches.

Descent: Described under Symmetry Spire, above.

Symmetry Spire, *Direct Jensen Ridge*

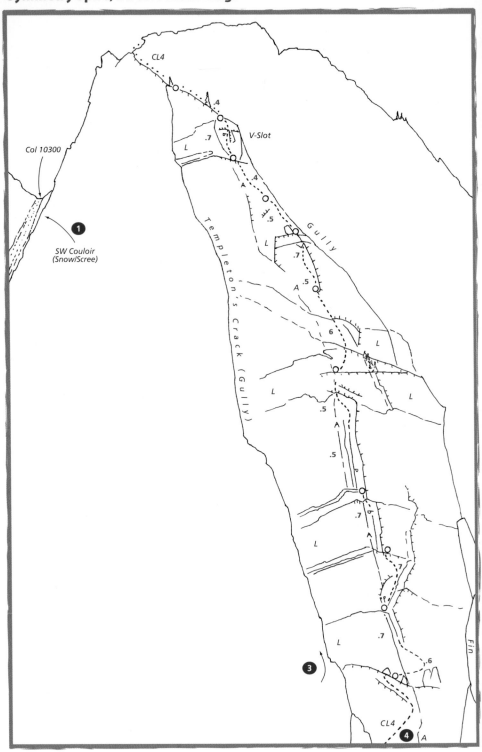

4. Direct Jensen Ridge (III 5.8) The Jensen Ridge forms the right (east) side of *Templeton's Crack* and is considerably more difficult than the *Southwest Ridge* route; however, the middle section of the climb degenerates into steep scrambling on less than wonderful rock. The route was pieced together by different parties between 1938 and 1953. The first free ascent of the entire ridge was completed by Willi Unsoeld, Mary Sylvander, and Steve Jervis on August 16, 1953.

The Route

From the bottom of *Durrance Ridge,* descend into the chimney of *Templeton's Crack* and traverse east onto the ridge. Traverse right to within 50 feet of the gully on the right side of the ridge, then work up and left to belay on a ledge. **Pitch 1:** Traverse right to some flakes, then cut back left to a vertical crack that is climbed to a ledge beneath a large overhang (5.7). **Pitch 2:** Work up under the roof, traverse right over the top of a large flake, then work up and left to belay on a ledge beside a left-facing dihedral. Move the belay to the corner of the dihedral. **Pitch 3:** Climb up toward a flake, then move back right and go straight up to the top of the dihedral (5.8). Belay in a deep alcove. **Pitch 4:** The next pitch may be climbed on either side of the crest. The left version ascends cracks in the left wall of a large dihedral (5.5). Exit the dihedral in a chimney, work up the face, and belay on a long ledge halfway up the ridge. **Pitch 5:** Climb steep slabs and belay at the bottom of a left-facing dihedral (5.6). **Pitch 6:** Climb slabs out and left from the dihedral, then veer back to the right and climb through a slot (5.7) to a good ledge. **Pitch 7:** Climb an easy lead up and slightly right to a stance on the crest (5.5). **Pitch 8:** Scramble up and left for a rope length or more and belay on a ledge left of the crest (5.4). **Pitch 9:** Work up and slightly left and climb an awkward V-slot through a roof (5.7+). Belay above where the angle eases off. **Pitch 10:** Climb a long moderate pitch that passes a small roof on the right (5.4). Scramble up to the west, intersect the final section of the *Southwest Ridge,* and continue to the summit.

   Rack: Full gear up to 2.5 inches.

   Descent: Described under Symmetry Spire, above.

5. East Ridge (II Class 4) No topo. The first ascent of Symmetry Spire was made via the *East Ridge* on August 20, 1929, by Fritiof Fryxell and Phil Smith. This highly visible ridge provides an excellent climb. It also may be used as a descent from the summit to avoid snow in the *Northeast Couloir.* Hike the Hanging Canyon Trail to Arrowhead Pool above Ribbon Cascade. Cross the stream west of the pool and gain a grassy shelf that leads out onto the east ridge, just above a minor

North Face of Symmetry Spire from Ramshead Lake, July 26, 2011

Ramshead Lake

summit called Sam's Tower. Follow the ridge about 1,000 feet to the summit.

Rack: This route is usually climbed without a rope. To err on the side of caution, bring a light rock rack up to 2 inches (and a rope).

Descent: Reverse the route or descend as described above.

6. Northwest Couloir (I Class 4, AI2+) This excellent alpine route was first climbed in conjunction with the *Northwest Ledges* by Fritiof Fryxell, Leland Horberg, Rudolph Edmund, William Cerderberg, Neuman Kerndt and Elof Petersen on July 13, 1931. Begin from the west end of Ramshead Lake. Cross the stream and climb a talus fan through a break in a low cliff. Scramble up and right, then work back left into the couloir. Climb snow or scree up the steep couloir to Col 10300 between Symmetry Spire and Symmetry Crags (to the west). From here you can climb the *Northwest Ledges* (Class 4) to the summit or descend the *Southwest Couloir* to routes on the south side. The *Northwest Couloir* may be used in conjunction with the Hanging Canyon Trail as an alternative to the standard *Southwest Couloir-Symmetry Couloir* descent. The upper couloir is quite steep. An ascent or descent on snow should not be underestimated.

Rack: An ice axe, mountain boots and crampons are needed in the couloir until late summer.

Descent: Reverse the route (carefully) or downclimb the East Ridge to avoid snow and return to Hanging Canyon.

CUBE POINT

Cube Point (9,600+ feet) is the prominent tooth-like summit on the long east ridge that descends from Symmetry Spire. The smaller summit just to the west is Sam's Tower. Cube Point takes its name from a large, angular block that forms the actual summit.

Approach: Hike the Hanging Canyon Trail to Arrowhead Pool on the shelf above Ribbon Cascade.

1. East Couloir (II Class 4) This is the easiest route to the summit, but it is more often used to reach the *East Ridge;* it also is the usual choice for descent. In early season it is a good snow climb. The first ascent is uncertain. Begin from the bench below and immediately east of Ribbon Falls. Hike southwest up a talus fan and enter the couloir that curves up around the east ridge of Cube Point. Follow the couloir around to the south side of the tower and climb to its end at a small notch. Turn north

Cube Point from the Northeast

and gain the crest. The final block may be scaled on its south or west side.

Rack: Ice axe and mountain boots until mid-summer.

Descent: Downclimb the *East Couloir* or go west and downclimb the *West Chimney* (a short rappel may be desired).

2. East Ridge (II 5.4) The *East Ridge* route on Cube Point is a Teton mini-classic. It is often used as an early season warm-up and features a sweeping snow couloir and excellent rock. The first ascent is uncertain. Follow the *East Couloir* (above) to where it narrows and curves around the bottom of the east ridge. Leave the snow and climb the ridge to a big ledge (Class 4). Climb a steep but well-protected pitch up excellent rock on the crest to where the angle eases off. Continue up the ridge to the almost level summit crest and scramble to the "cube," which is most easily climbed on either its south or west side.

Rack: Light rock rack up to 2 inches. Ice axe and mountain boots until mid–summer.

Descent: Downclimb the *East Couloir* or the *West Chimney*.

3. North Face Center (II 5.4) The history of this route is unknown. The description is based on an ascent by Richard Rossiter, Lynn Householder, and Ike Gayfield on October 4, 1975. The main value of this route is that it is an easy way to reach the summit

without snow travel. Begin from the bench above Arrowhead Pool and contour southeast to the lower right side of the north face. Scramble up onto a ledge to get started. **Pitch 1:** Work up and left along a ramp, then climb up and right to a sloping shelf with trees. **Pitch 2:** Climb up and right along a norrow ledge, then work up and left to the summit ridge just east of the "cube," which is most easily scaled on either its south or west side.

Rack: Light rock gear up to 2 inches.

Descent: Downclimb the *East Couloir* or the *West Chimney*.

4. West Chimney (II 5.1) This short route was first climbed by Paul Petzoldt, Joseph Hawkes, and Bernard Nobel on July 6, 1940. Begin from the shelf above Arrowhead Pool and scramble to the notch between Cube Point and Sam's Tower. Climb a chockstone chimney and exit left to a narrow ridge that leads to the summit block. Stay left and climb the northwest side of the summit block.

Rack: Light rock rack up to 2 inches.

Descent: Downclimb the route. A short rappel may be desired.

BAXTER PINNACLE

There are very few "short subjects" in the Tetons, that is, compact rock climbs with easy access. Among such leisurely outings, Baxter Pinnacle (8,560+ feet) is as short as they get.

Baxter Pinnacle. View from the Horse Trail Showing the *South Ridge* Route.

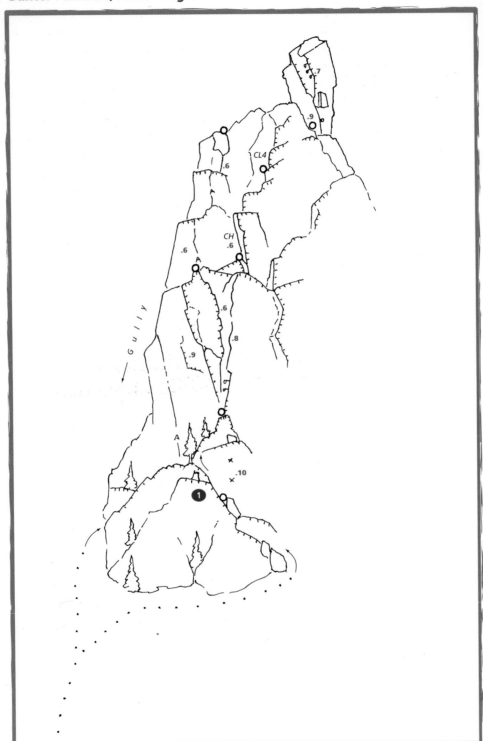